Of Dutch Ways

Of Dutch Ways

by Helen Colijn

PERENNIAL LIBRARY

Harper & Row, Publishers
New York, Cambridge, Philadelphia, San Francisco
London, Mexico City, São Paulo, Singapore, Sydney

OF DUTCH WAYS. Copyright © 1980 by Dillon Press, Inc. All rights reserved. Printed in the United States of America. No part of this book may be used or reproduced in any manner whatsoever without written permission except in the case of brief quotations embodied in critical articles and reviews. For information address HarperCollins Publishers, 10 East 53rd Street, New York, NY 10022.

First HarperPerennial edition published 1984. Reissued in 1991.

Library of Congress Cataloging-in-Publication Data

Colijn, Helen.
    Of Dutch ways.

    Reprint. Originally published: Minneapolis, Minn.: Dillon Press, c1980.
    Bibliography: p.
    Includes index.
    1. Netherlands. I. Title.
DJ18.C62   1984   949.2   83-48338
ISBN 0-06-092250-8

92 93 94 95 MPC 10 9 8 7 6

CONTENTS

For Madelyn

FOREWORD

SOME YEARS AGO Helen Colijn was in my office and asked if I knew of a book on The Netherlands for Americans in a tour group she was escorting. She wanted "something that explains the Eighty Years War and the House of Orange, and how we came by all those marvelous paintings, and why we have subsidized schools for different religious groups—and it should be fun to read." I couldn't think of such a book, and now Helen has written it.

With a few deft strokes she has described our complex political system, our unique educational system, and the problems of living in a country that, except for Bangladesh, is the most densely populated in the world. She has also shared her personal experiences in culture, sports, and everyday living.

All this is conveyed from the vantage point of the insider who was born and raised in The Netherlands and returns every year for an updated look. But as a person who has lived abroad for well-nigh forty years, she knows she should capture the little things we take for granted but outsiders find strange, like eating *speculaas* cookies on bread and buying potatoes peeled.

The result of this dual viewpoint is an immensely useful book, written with verve and affection and a wise choice of topics. *Of Dutch Ways* will enhance any tourist's stay by providing a better understanding of what makes the Dutch tick. A newly arrived foreigner taking up residence in The Netherlands will also welcome the diverse information. So will anyone living beyond our borders who's interested in Dutch ways, not the least being the immigrant or descendant for whom this book is intended.

J. N. Strijkers
Director, National Bureau for Tourism
The Hague

Provinces:
1 Friesland
2 Groningen
3 Drenthe
4 Overijssel
5 Gelderland
6 Limburg
7 North Brabant
8 Utrecht
9 Zeeland
10 South Holland
11 North Holland

North Sea

Terschelling

Wadden Sea

Leeuwarden

Dam

Hindeloopen

Wieringermeer

Stavoren

Northeast Polder

11

Projected Markerwaard

Volendam

Marken

Flevoland

IJssel

Amsterdam

The Hague

10

Rotterdam

8

5

9

7

Rhine

Meuse

6

2

3

4

THE
NETHERLANDS

Maastricht

INTRODUCTION

IN A SENSE this book has been a-growing since long ago, when I went on Sunday walks with my parents and two sisters in Holland. I came to know every sand dune, beach, polder, and dike within a ten-mile radius of our home in The Hague.

When I was seventeen and my parents moved to the Dutch East Indies, I went to live with my paternal grandparents. My grandfather, Dr. Hendrikus Colijn, was prime minister for the fourth time and also walked on Sundays. As I accompanied him, this kindly man explained Dutch politics, which were as complex in the 1930s as they are today.

I learned about the Nazi occupation of my homeland from friends and relatives, since I spent three and a half years of World War II in Japanese concentration camps in the East Indies, as did my sisters and parents. Father died.

When my mother, sisters, and I immigrated to California at the war's end, I thought this meant good-bye to The Netherlands, but soon I was making annual trips back and gathering lecture material. During a ten-year period I organized European tours for American teenagers and adults and found myself discoursing to my charges about the masterpieces in Dutch museums and the wonders of the artificial Dutch landscape.

After my American-born daughter settled in Amsterdam and I continued to commute across the Atlantic, I decided that there must be a reason for so much Holland in my life. I have made generous and loving use of it in the writing of *Of Dutch Ways*.

To make room for the people, Dutch water wizards have turned the sea to land. Eastern Flevoland, the area shown here, "fell dry" in 1957.

CHAPTER 1

A CROWDED LAND

IF YOU ASK TWO Dutch persons, "which country are you from?" one may answer, "The Netherlands" and the other "Holland." Both mean the same tiny land, all of 72 miles wide and 180 long, nestled in the northwestern tip of the European continent between Germany, Belgium, and the North Sea.

The Kingdom of The Netherlands is its official name. Holland is merely the name of a province that centuries ago was the richest and most powerful in The Netherlands. As the years passed, the part was taken for the whole, and the entire country was called Holland. The name annoyed the Dutch of other provinces, who had never felt part of Holland. Many still don't. They go to Amsterdam in the province of North Holland or to The Hague in South Holland and say, "I'm going to Holland," as if they were going to a foreign country.

The Kingdom of The Netherlands is one of the flattest, smallest, and most densely populated nations in the world. Except for a few tiny bumps, the entire country is flat as a pancake, and on this little patch of dry land live fourteen million people. Half of the land area has been cleverly captured from marshes, rivers, and sea and made into dike-girded polders.

These polders are so low—many below sea level—that the Dutch must constantly be on the alert lest the water snatch back their hard-won soil. And there is plenty of water to be leery of. In the north hefty dikes shield the polders and in the west, rows of dunes. One-sixth of the nation is water: rivers like the Scheldt, Meuse, Rhine, and IJssel, their tributaries and estuaries, shipping canals, polder canals, lakes, man-made reservoirs, and the inland Wadden Sea. Men and women stand guard at hundreds of sluices and twenty-three hundred electric pumping stations that supersede the historic windmills. They pull knobs, turn handles, press buttons and, with much planning and forethought, control the water in the waterways by letting it in here and out somewhere else.

There are a thousand miles of sea and river dikes. The boy who put his finger in a hole in a dike never existed, but he does symbolize the need for vigilance. Water trickling through a breach quickly becomes a gushing stream and then a roaring flood. When the tide rises high or the river is full and a fierce winter gale blows, volunteer dike guards with walkie-talkies pace the dikes and scan for danger spots.

"It's artificial country," wrote the Italian Edmondo de Amicis in an 1880 travel book. "The Dutch made it; it exists because the Dutch preserve it; it will vanish whenever the Dutch shall abandon it."

This man-made polder country is in the Low Netherlands, comprising roughly the five coastal provinces. From the Belgian border northward they are: Zeeland ("Sea Land"), sea-washed islands only recently closed off from the sea and connected with the rest of The Netherlands by bridges and dams; South Holland, where the country reaches its lowest point at twenty-two feet below sea level; North Holland; and "at the top of the country," Friesland and Groningen. The six Wadden Islands that lie like a crescent-shaped diadem above the northern Wadden Sea are also reckoned among the Low Netherlands.

It is a curious sensation to stand in a Dutch polder. You

look *up* at the surrounding dike. Above its grassy slope smokestacks and sails glide by on vessels you do not see. In Lake Haarlem polder near Amsterdam, a freeway dips under a dike and adjacent canal. As you approach the underpass, a big barge may chug overhead.

From a road-topped dike, on the other hand, you look *down* on the pastures and the cultivated fields. Straight, narrow drainage ditches cut them in rectangles and squares. You are reminded of a geometric painting by the Dutch abstractionist, Piet Mondrian, who was probably inspired by the polders. The horizon is flat, wide, and very low. Seven-eighths of what you see is sky, perhaps filled with billowing clouds.

Not only painters have been taken with the polders. The poet Hendrik Marsman lovingly describes his native landscape this way:

Thinking of Holland
I see wide rivers
slowly winding
through endless lowland;
rows of delicate
filigreed poplars,
plumelike, high
on the horizon stand;
snugly ensconced
in limitless space
farms lie scattered
all over the land;
trees and villages,
truncated towers,
churches and elms
form a pattern so grand;
the sky hangs low
and slowly the sun

is wrapped in vapors
of varying grey;
and in all regions
the voice of the water
herald of danger
is heard with dismay.

Few Dutch think about the water threat, although more than two-thirds of the population live on vulnerable, low-lying land.

The remaining one-third live in the High Netherlands, where the terrain undulates occasionally and produces little hills the Dutch call mountains. The Empire State Building in New York City exceeds the height of the Vaalser Mountain, the country's highest point, by almost two hundred feet.

The High Netherlands covers the approximate area of the six inland provinces. Starting again in the south, they are Limburg, North Brabant, Utrecht, Gelderland, Overijssel, and Drenthe. Here fields are lined with hedges instead of ditches, and there are sandy heaths and woods of pine and beech. The horizons are lumpy. The Dutch call this landscape "furnished."

In the High Netherlands is most of the country's vacant land, some of which has been set aside in nature preserves. Droves of Dutch come here to enjoy the out-of-doors and soak up the sunshine when the fickle weather favors them.

The weather, in fact, is a favorite topic of conversation and for good reason. Sunshine comes all in a bunch during several glorious halcyon weeks or daily in short spurts between rain squalls. Some cautious Dutch never leave the house without a raincoat or an umbrella. The rainfall is moderate—twenty-eight inches annually—but it is unpredictable. Whatever the time of year, a visitor may expect pouring rain day after day or no rain at all.

Something unfortunate has happened to the winter weather in recent years. Since the early 1960s the average temperature has been thirty-six degrees, and it has rarely been cold enough to freeze over the canals so the Dutch can skate. Instead, long dreary spells of dry but overcast skies have alternated with mushy days of hail, wet snow, rain, and in the country, dense fog. Driving becomes hazardous then, and even the most ardent motorists take the train.

During the shortest winter days the sun rises at eight and sets at four, and when the long summer days are at their peak, you can still read a newspaper by daylight at ten at night. Summer temperatures average sixty degrees. During the rare times that the mercury climbs to ninety, the Dutch talk about a heatwave.

The one aspect of Dutch weather that is predictable is the wind since there is little in that flat land to stop it. That's why most of the sidewalk cafés have glass windscreens at the sides. The coastal dunes are planted with marram grass so the wind won't carry them off, and sunbathers rent colorful canvas windscreens to prop up in the sand.

Windy or not, the white sandy beaches that line the dunes are jampacked when the summer sun is shining. The most popular ones are those of Scheveningen and Zandvoort, which draw crowds from the country's most crowded area, Rim City Holland.

Randstad ("Rim City") is a word coined in the 1950s for the horseshoe-shaped area between the North Sea and the towns of Amsterdam, Utrecht, and Rotterdam. In the Rim City nearly half the Dutch population lives on 16 percent of the country's land area, and for this reason it has been the focus of intensive national planning since World War II. What did the Dutch do to prevent the Rim City towns from growing together into one huge urban blob? What did they do with farms, tourist attractions, and long-established busi-

nesses and industry, numerous government centers, all
mixed up in this very small space?

Limited decentralization of private and government enter-
prises provided one answer, but a large-scale exodus from
the Rim City was impractical. Horticulture and agriculture
were allowed to stay as "green buffer zones" between the
growing towns. Just beyond the city limits the omnipresent
black and white cows graze on lush green grass. An
occasional windmill, now preserved as a national monument, swooshes its mighty arms and pumps water from a
polder ditch not far from a giant factory.

The Rim City has four main nuclei, each with its own
distinctive character. Amsterdam, the nation's capital and
center of finance, has nearly a million inhabitants and is the
liveliest and most permissive town in The Netherlands. "In
Amsterdam everything goes." At the mouth of the Rhine,
vital trade route for western Europe, lies hard-working
Rotterdam. Its port, known by the name of Europort, has
surpassed New York as the world's largest, and within
Europort is a huge industrial complex where oil is refined and
bulk commodities are stored for shipment all over the globe.
Although Amsterdam is the capital, the Dutch government
meets in The Hague, a sedate town of poise and protocol.
Utrecht, quietest of the four, is perhaps the most distinguished. Near the cathedral, which was supposedly started in
691, are Roman foundations that prove the town was already
there nineteen hundred years ago. Utrecht is a major rail and
road junction and hosts international fairs. With these four
separate nuclei, Rim City Holland will never have the
problems of a megapolis like New York or London, where
traffic, supplies, and people all have to flow ever farther to
and from one central core.

The Rim City is cluttered nonetheless. Right after the war
the solution seemed to be moving people outside the Rim to

live. Soon the surrounding provinces began to lose their rural charm as they became crowded with people, and commuters caused traffic jams on Rim City highways. The current trend is to have people live close to their work.

To coax people back to the Rim City, the Dutch are making old towns more livable by restoring old dwellings with character rather than tearing them down to make room for modern, impersonal flats. Planners leave narrow streets as pedestrian malls instead of ripping them out in favor of wide streams of concrete. For the overflow of people from the towns they are building self-contained growth nuclei in the polders that do not infringe on the designated green buffer zones.

The Dutch approach their problems conscientiously and with methods well thought out beforehand.

To characterize them further, with all the reservations customary in such matters, the word "individualist" immediately comes to mind. The Dutch like to do things their own way. And once set on a course, they will stick to their goal with a determination that some call stubbornness. The long struggle against the water is supposed to account for this Dutch quality.

They are persistent in their beliefs, too, and easily irked when they have to put up for long with dissenting opinions within their group. Then they prefer to start a new organization without disbanding the old one. "Our compartment mentality," the Dutch call it. Many seem content only in their own pigeonhole, surrounded by others with the same outlook on life, but they gladly step out of their compartments and join those who think differently to shoulder a common task.

And they are tolerant of those in other compartments. "Live and let live!" is a motto worn by long experience in The Netherlands. In the sixteenth century the Dutch stopped burning witches and beheading heretics long before the surrounding countries abandoned the practice. Instead, the Dutch offered asylum to those persecuted for their faith. A Dutch person with the last name of Cordozo probably has a Jewish ancestor who fled Portugal during the Inquisition. The name Boucher or Labouchère suggests ancestors who were Protestant Huguenots from France.

In recent times the Dutch have shown great indulgence toward alternate lifestyles. Not so long ago, young foreign travelers were allowed to bed down in their sleeping bags on the base of the monument for the fallen in World War II on Amsterdam's Dam Square. Now they are provided with sleep-inns in old warehouses. Sex boutiques, nudist beaches, prostitution within certain zones, and the sale of marijuana are all permitted for those who want it. The prices of cannabis were once announced daily over the radio, but many Dutch felt this was stretching tolerance a bit too far!

"Isn't it just like us?" one citizen remarked. "We never like to pay more than we have to, not even for our sins."

The Dutch have always had a reputation for thrift. The former dearth of land to live on and their long history of trading may have something to do with this. Waste is frowned upon, and tastes are generally simple. There are few ostentatious homes, flashy cars, and flamboyant clothes. Still, these people careful with money are generous givers.

One and a half percent of the national income goes to underdeveloped countries. In the private sector action groups, of which the Dutch have an infinite number, solicit support for flood and famine victims far away. Televised pledge marathons collect huge sums for the handicapped and needy in their own country.

By and large the Dutch are homebodies. Although hyper-modern rooms with stark white walls and pillows on the floor do exist, the majority of interiors are what the Dutch call *gezellig*, a term the Dutch dictionary defines as "pleasant, cozy, and entertaining."

"Why don't you come over for an evening of gezellig talk?" is a much-heard invitation.

A typical living room has lots of potted plants in the window and lots of framed photos on the walls. A rack shows off hand-decorated china, commemorative plates, or antique pewter dishes while a cabinet displays silver curios. Piles of books, newspapers, and ash trays or other souvenirs from foreign trips are scattered over several small tables, which may be covered with little Persian-style red rugs. There's a profusion of overstuffed chairs and a coffee table. Add to this a sideboard with a tray holding a teapot tucked under a cozy and cups and saucers that are often different for each member of the family, and you have a room that is truly gezellig.

Gezellig can also apply to a family that plays and works together in fun and harmony and always has room for a guest. That is, someone the family knows. Strangers are not usually invited home, not out of unfriendliness but because of an inborn Dutch reserve. A few years ago, when I called a Dutch friend to say hello from a distant, unknown relative in California who planned to call on him, he wondered how to entertain the guest. I suggested dinner at home, but he asked, "How can I do that? I don't even know him!" His American visitor would first be entertained in a restaurant.

An exception is Get in Touch with the Dutch, an organization whose members will gladly invite a stranger from abroad. The group tries to match backgrounds or interests. And young people are not held back by all that old-fashioned Dutch reserve, either.

Caring as they do about their homes, the Dutch have earned an international reputation for domestic cleanliness. William Temple, a seventeenth-century English ambassador to The Netherlands, told a story in his memoirs about a maid who greeted him at the door of a wealthy burgher's home. Noting the ambassador's dirty shoes, she lifted him in her arms, carried him over her just-polished hallway, put him down, and said, "The mistress will be glad to see you."

Domestic help, with or without strong arms, is rare now, and the Dutch passion for scrubbing floors, stoops, and sidewalks with soap and water is also on the wane. Urban women go over the house lightly as they pursue careers and hobbies. Frequent visitors notice a difference. The towns of The Netherlands, particularly those of the Rim City, do not look as spic and span as they used to. In the country, where old habits die more slowly, there is still much window cleaning and stoop washing going on, often on Saturday so the house will look its best on the Sabbath.

It must be said here that the Dutch national character is much influenced by regional differences. Not only do "typical" Dutch traits differ from region to region, but so do Dutch physical features. In rural areas families have lived for generations in the same village and married only local folks. Tall, blue-eyed blondes are common in the north while "below the rivers" in the south, the locals tend to be of a smaller stature and have dark hair and dark eyes. In the cities there is generally a mixture, which may include those of partly Malayan ancestry from the days before 1949 when the huge archipelago of the Republic of Indonesia was still a Dutch colony and intermarriage between the Dutch and Indonesians occurred. Now some Dutch have smooth, jet black hair and slightly oriental features. One hundred thirty-five thousand men, women, and children migrated from Surinam until 1976, when the colony regained its independence. These Surinamers are mostly blacks, and they, too, are Dutch citizens. The typical Dutch look exists no more than the typical American look.

The official language of The Netherlands is *Nederlands*.

A question the Dutch may resent is whether Dutch is a dialect of German (*Deutsch*). Because of the similarity of the two words, the assumption is understandable. In fact, both "Dutch" and "Deutsch" are derived from *Diets*, a medieval language which the two peoples once spoke in varying dialects. Dutch and German, however, have developed their own linguistic identities. Although similar in some respects, they are definitely not the same.

In Friesland, Frisian has recently gained the status of a second official language. It's spoken by four hundred thousand Frisians. Names of towns are posted in Frisian and Dutch, and many schools are also bilingual.

Twenty-five dialects are still alive in the little country and are now enjoying renewed attention. The Commission for the Modernization of the Mother Tongue studies the learning ability of first graders who have to switch from their native dialect to standard Dutch. In Drenthe groups meet regularly to compile words for a Drenthe dictionary. The Limburg periodical *Veldeke* promotes literature in the vernacular.

The dialects affect the way Nederlands is spoken. As you travel below the rivers, for example, you can't help noticing, even if you don't speak a word of Dutch, that the *g* sounds soft and soothing rather than guttural and harsh as it does in the north.

You may well find a journey either "above" or "below the rivers" a delightful adventure. The country is built on a small scale. Wherever you want to go is never far away, and whatever you see never lasts long enough to be boring. Still, 70 percent of this crowded land is grass or under cultivation. Muted tones of greens and grays are often bathed in a wondrous light that, when reflected in the water, makes all small things seem bigger. The fields are neat and orderly. Nothing is left to the whim of nature or the negligence of man.

Detail of *The Company of Captain Frans Banning Cocq*, popularly known as *Night Watch*, by Rembrandt.

CHAPTER 2

THE GOLDEN AGE

IN THE 1600s the importance of The Netherlands was quite out of proportion to its size.

Intrepid Dutch sea captains on tiny sailing vessels discovered faraway places and gave them Dutch names. New Zealand was called after the province of Zeeland, and Tasmania after Captain Abel Tasman. Cape Horn at the tip of South America took its name from the town of Hoorn. At the other end of the world, a Javanese town, Jakarta, was renamed Batavia after the Batavi, a tribe that lived in the Lowlands in Roman times.

Dutch traders, already old hands at buying silk and wine in the Mediterranean, lumber and grain in the Baltic, and wool in England, now ventured all the way to China for porcelain, and to the Moluccas for cloves, pepper, and cinnamon.

Dutch trade and shipping became profitable. When spice-bearing ships returned, stockholders of the Dutch East Indies Company received dividends of 40 to 50 percent. The merchants' new wealth enabled a flowering of the arts and sciences unequalled in the annals of the Dutch before or since.

The Golden Age had a difficult birth. From 1568 to 1648 the Dutch were embroiled in a searing war with their feudal sovereign, the King of Spain. When he came to the throne in 1555, King Philip II packed Margaret, his half-sister and the Duchess of Parma, off to Brussels as his regentess.

Isolating himself in his Spanish palaces and the monasteries he visited for retreats, he nourished his dreams: the supremacy of Spain and the supremacy of the Roman Catholic Church.

In the seventeen Lowlands provinces then united under Philip's rule, he had Spanish noblemen appointed to influential positions coveted by the local gentry. He had Protestants brought before a Spanish court of inquisition and tortured. After forced confessions they were shot, beheaded, hanged from the gallows, or burned at the stake.

Lowlands noblemen, Prince William of Orange among them, complained to Margaret of Philip's absolutist ways and the dreadful persecutions. "I cannot approve that sovereigns want to rule over the conscience of their subjects," William said.

This Catholic German prince had inherited the principality of Orange in France and properties in the Lowlands. He envisioned all the seventeen provinces ruled by Philip who was, after all, everyone's God-given sovereign, but with the counsel of the States-General, convened in Brussels, where deputies of each province discussed matters of general interest. The meddling Spanish dons had to go, their jobs filled by local noblemen. And there must be freedom of religion.

Before he died at the hands of a religious fanatic in 1584, William's beliefs, both political and religious, had changed. The Northern Lowlands had proclaimed themselves independent, ruled by the States-General, and he had left the Catholic church. His last words were, "Oh God, have pity on my poor people." They grieved for William, champion of their Protestant faith. Father of the Fatherland, they called him. He never saw the glory that was to come to his little, war-torn nation, the Republic of the Seven United Netherlands.

Three generations of Dutch suffered from war on their

home soil. Poorly paid, ill-fed mercenary soldiers from both sides marauded the countryside, plundered storehouses, and raped the local women. The side that held the towns had the riches. Prize towns—those with thriving trade or with an industry like textiles—were besieged for months by Spanish or Dutch troops.

To save beleaguered towns, leaders of the revolt made agonizing decisions. Knowing the devastation that would be endured by Dutch farmers, they ordered sluices opened and dikes breached to flood the land. The Spanish took one look at the surging water and ran.

Water saved Alkmaar in 1573—a turning point in the war. Water saved Leiden in 1574. The desperate townspeople, cut off from food supplies, ate boiled cowhide and rats and pleaded with the mayor to surrender. He then spoke the historic words every Dutch child learns in school, "Cut my body in pieces and distribute it as far as it will go—we will not give up."

Displaced persons, disabled soldiers, and refugees from religious persecution crowded into the towns. Prices went up and up. Many people went hungry. Epidemics of plague and cholera killed thousands. Hoping to escape the horrors at home, Dutchmen volunteered for the republic's navy or the merchant ships. Aboard they suffered from inedible food, disease, atrocious punishments like keel-hauling, and the continual threat of having even unarmed craft shot at by enemy cannon, set afire, and sunk.

The merchants fared well in the war. When the Spaniards took Antwerp, in what is now Belgium, the Dutch no longer traded there, and the town languished. Skilled Antwerp craftsmen took refuge in Holland, most prosperous of the seven independent provinces, and especially in Amsterdam, Holland's most prosperous town.

War stepped up the need for Dutch-built ships, sails, and ropes.

The merchants were never too particular to whom they sold. When a Dutch town was besieged, the Spanish needed vinegar to cool their cannon, and Dutch merchants sold it to them. "The Dutch would trade with the devil in hell," an old saying goes, "if they weren't afraid their sails would burn."

Wartime piracy was legitimate in those days. To raise money to continue the war, the national government or a town council issued a letter of marque. Businessmen pooled money to equip a pirate fleet, and the spoils were later divided among the captains and crew, the letter-issuing authority, and the financial backers.

Pirate captains were national heroes.Dutch children still sing about the admiral who cornered and looted a Spanish flotilla laden with silver from South American mines:

> Piet Hein, Piet Hein,
> Small is his name,
> Great is his fame.
> He captured the silver fleet,
> The silver fleet from Spain.

Enthusiasm for the war waned. Fighting declined into haggling over treaty terms. At last, in 1648, the weary state of war gave over to the full blossoming of the Golden Age.

During the long, long war the persecuted Protestant minority had worked its way to the top, but the one-time goal of religious freedom was forgotten in the struggle. Now powerful Calvinists expected non-Calvinists to practice their religion out of sight and not to hold public office or to vote. When Limburg and Brabant, two predominantly Catholic provinces, were added to the republic, they were required to pay taxes without having voting rights.

The merchants who had the money became ruling burghers of the Dutch nation. Their austere religion and often narrow, middle-class mentality put a stamp on the arts that was different from that of previous art patrons, the Catholic Church and flamboyant noble courts.

The burghers commissioned still lifes to display their opulence. An oil by Willem Kalf shows an intricately chiseled jug of silver, a transparent blue china plate, and a costly lemon imported from the south of France. If you look carefully in the lower right-hand corner, you'll see an open fob watch that gives a little moral message to the burghers: all earthly goods are transient.

The Protestant burghers were against glorification of the saints, of course, but they had nothing against a little glorification of themselves and commissioned portraits of themselves, their wives, and their children in their finest clothes.

Frans Hals painted a distinguished matron, Maritge Voogt Claesdr. She shines in rich velvet, silk, and imported Russian beaver. Her face, framed by the customary tight-fitting cap, floats on a cascade of finely pleated white ruff. A coat of arms, once an exclusive attribute of the nobility, catches your eye. In her lap she holds a gold-clasped Bible, maybe to tell one and all that she's a Protestant.

Cultural emphasis shifted from heavenly to earthly matters. Golden Age painters show us a whole gamut of ordinary people doing ordinary things. Johannes Vermeer's pensive kitchen maid pours milk from a jug. Pieter de Hoogh's mother delouses a child's head. Jan Steen's robust baker proudly shows his loaves of freshly baked bread. In Steen's cluttered tavern and household scenes, common people laugh, eat, drink, and flirt, while dogs bark and chickens strut over a floor littered with broken eggshells.

Judith Leyster's joyful lute player has an earthy quality about him. You just know he doesn't come from one of the stuffy patrician homes! Leyster was a student of Frans Hals and the foremost female painter of her time. Several paintings credited to Hals were later discovered to be Leyster's.

Painters often worked on speculation and hung works in their studios where buyers from abroad, charmed by the Dutch landscapes with huge skies and wide, flat horizons dotted with windmills, bought them as an investment.

Dutch ice scenes must also have been popular because so many were painted. One of the best-selling ice painters was deaf-mute Hendrick Avercamp. In his paintings richly dressed citizens talk in a huddle on the ice, a beggar asks for alms, men and women skate vigorously, a boy kicks a ball with a stick that looks like a golf club, and a mother pushes a child in a sled.

The burghers wanted their good works immortalized, too. Especially fashionable were group paintings commissioned by the board members of charitable institutions. Men and women who sponsored a private leper house, an old men's home, or an orphanage would sit smugly for the paintings that would hang in the boardrooms of their favorite charity. Each person paid a proportionate share.

A civic guard piece was commissioned by the officers of a town's militia to adorn the club room next to the shooting range. Because every man was eager to stand out as much as the next one, the painter felt compelled to make a stiff composition. All figures are frozen in a row or awkwardly arranged around a banquet table. Their bright costumes trimmed with gold braid and gilded buttons, their colorful sashes, and their jaunty wide-brimmed hats with enormous plumes are all shown in impartial, painstaking detail.

These paintings are so large that today's Dutch have found many of them to be a problem to hang for public display. Fourteen huge canvases featuring the Amsterdam Civic Guard are exhibited high along the walls of a "museum street," a covered passage near the Amsterdam Historic Museum. A museum guard strolls discreetly up and down the thoroughfare that runs between Spui and Sint Luciënsteeg.

The most famous civic guard piece hangs in that treasure house of Golden Age paintings, the National Gallery in Amsterdam. The painting is Rembrandt van Rijn's twelve-by-fourteen-foot *The Company of Captain Frans Banning Cocq.* We know it as *Night Watch,* the name later given to the painting when it had grown dark with dirt and layers of protective varnish. (It has since been restored to its original luster.)

The men are getting ready for a parade while Captain Frans gives directions. They load powder in a musket, blow the extra powder off, and try out a twelve-foot pike for size. Some of the figures are far more visible than others since Rembrandt was using chiaroscuro, a brand-new effect of light and shadow imported from Italy. Persistent tales that the men in the shade were furious and wanted their money back have been recently refuted.

Art critics are still speculating about the little girl in a golden dress with a chicken hanging from her belt. She may be the company's mascot, a curious child who had just come back from the market, or a playful whim of the master to distract attention from the pompous Captain Frans.

For its time *Night Watch* was unconventional—a departure from the prescribed style and forms that painter-craftsmen were "supposed" to produce. Rembrandt risked his own ideas and got away with them. "I feel this painting will outlast all its competitors," fellow-painter Samuel van Hoogstraten wrote in 1678. "It's so picturesque of conception, so dashing in actions, and so powerful that it makes all other [civic guard] pieces look like playing cards." But he did add, "Still, I wish he had lit more lights in it."

Except for his early paintings, Rembrandt signed only his first name. (Van Rijn referred to the Rhine in Leiden where his father owned a windmill.) A prolific worker, he completed two thousand drawings, three hundred etchings, and six hundred and fifty oil paintings. His penetrating self-portraits take the measure of genius from a self-assured, dashing young man to a reflective sixty-year-old. There are portraits of his mother, his son Titus—the only one of four children who survived infancy—and Saskia, his wife who died before she was thirty. Little is known about their life together, but when you see Rembrandt's touching drawing of Saskia wearing a big straw hat and holding a flower in her hand, you feel that the man who sketched her was in love.

He became rich by his paintings but squandered his money and had to leave his handsome Amsterdam house on Breestraat. It's now a museum for his etchings and a fine sample of the houses well-to-do Golden Age burghers built.

Rembrandt's brick house is four stories high and, by Amsterdam standards, wide—"five windows across." A flight of stone steps lined by an iron railing leads to a massive front door painted dark green. Under the roof jut two pulley beams, still distinctive features of Amsterdam homes. In the past, a pulley hoisted merchandise to the owner's warehouse in the attic, but now you walk in a street and see a piano or a sofa dangling from a sturdy rope until it slowly disappears through a window. This is an easier method of transport than struggling with large pieces on steep, narrow stairs. The houses the burghers built during the Golden Age still give Amsterdam its distinctive air. Many are skinny, only "three windows across," to minimize the building cost. In the inner city all houses have foundations built of poles sunk into the soggy soil to a depth of at least thirty feet. "The City drifts amid pools and marshes, but the weight of its many buildings is borne by a forest of trees," a professor said in 1632 in an inaugural speech at the *Athenaeum Illustre*, the future university of Amsterdam. The "trees" mustn't dry out or they'll rot, and the Amsterdam municipal water company is forever opening and closing canal sluices to keep the piles wet.

The largest pile-supported building—13,659 piles to be exact—is the palace on Dam Square. Seldom used now, it was once a bustling town hall. The burghers must have cast all notions of thrift and soberness aside when they accepted Jacob van Campen's design. The neoclassical interior, inspired by Palladio, has marble floors and walls and Corinthian columns—an extravagant place to conduct the town's business! But "the eighth wonder of the world," as tourists called it then, did credit to a town that was the richest in Europe.

Seventeenth-century Dutch Protestants didn't have to build many new churches because they had confiscated the Catholic ones. As Catholic Amsterdammers celebrated Mass out of sight on the top floor of a private home (listed as "Our Lord in the Attic" among current tourist attractions), Protestant Amsterdammers worshiped a few blocks away in the Old Church the Catholics built in the fourteenth century.

Not surprisingly, considering the triumph of Calvinism, the Bible was the most widely read book in the Golden Age. The version translated in the 1630s enriched the Dutch language just as the King James version did English; it also helped establish uniformity among many different dialects. This translation, "faithfully rendered from the original languages in our Dutch at the order of the high and mighty gentlemen of the States-General of the United Netherlands," as stated on the title page, is still read daily in orthodox Protestant homes.

The homilies of Jacob Cats, a favorite among pious burghers, have not stood the test of time as well. "Father Cats's" rhymes ooze morality, thrift, and down-to-earth advice about anything from making love to an unwilling husband to instructions in personal hygiene such as "Wash your hands and teeth, perhaps your feet, but your head under no circumstances." His well-intended teachings are no longer in print, but in many bookstores you'll still find the verse of the Golden Age poet, Joost van den Vondel. Some of his dramas and political allegories are required reading in Dutch high school classes.

The Golden Age also nurtured an interest in science, and Dutch names became bywords in academic circles abroad. Willem Bleau and his sons printed a famous twelve-volume atlas, copies of which are the rarest of treasures today, since most of the copper plates were lost in a fire. Christiaan Huygens perfected a telescope and discovered the rings around Saturn. He proffered new ideas about gravity and dynamics and developed the wave theory of light that is the foundation of modern optical science.

Huygens also designed a pendulum clock that fills a Dutch need to this day. Many don't consider a home *gezellig* without the ticktock of the grandfather clock or a smaller pendulum model gracing the mantel or hung on the wall.

Antoni van Leeuwenhoek invented a simple microscope. He saw creatures 270 times larger than their actual size and drew red blood cells, bacteria, and the propagation of fleas. The kings of England, Prussia, and Poland and anyone who was anybody in the scientific world came to his house in Delft to see the grandeur of God's creation in a drop of water.

Jan Swammerdam used the new invention to further entomology. He dissected, prepared, and cataloged some three thousand insects. "One is surprised," he wrote, "about the towering shoulders of an elephant or the mane of a lion; but nature is nowhere more perfect than in the smallest things." He spent a day trying to blow up a fly or rinsing the fat out of a caterpillar to study its innards. He spent days peering at the intestine of a bee. Nothing was too insignificant for Swammerdam. "Although the snail is a dirty and slippery little animal," he observed, "it is remarkable for those who explore the works of the Lord."

Hugo de Groot, also known as Hugo Grotius, was a child prodigy who entered the University of Leiden at eleven and received his law degree at fifteen. In a sad political dispute that started with splitting hairs about predestination, de Groot was imprisoned for life in Loevestein Castle. He escaped from the moat-girded, walled fortress in a bookcase that is now on view in The Netherlands history room of the National Gallery. Hugo must have been a small man or very uncomfortable while being smuggled out.

De Groot and his family fled to France, where he wrote the book for which he became internationally famous, *De Iure Belli ac Pacis* ("On the Law of War and Peace"). He had no use for piracy at sea, a favorite practice of his time, nor for wars of expansion. As for "just" wars, he affirmed that they should be conducted humanely in regard to private persons and their property. Three centuries later, World War I belligerents still consulted his book to settle arguments about war damages.

Baruch Spinoza, the son of Portuguese Jewish immigrants, is perhaps the most widely know Dutch philosopher. He was brought up to be a teacher in the Jewish faith, but as a young man he began to have doubts about his religion. "Where in the Talmud is it written," he asked, "that man is immortal?" And he dared to affirm that "God is everywhere; everything that exists, including man, is part of God."

The synagogue offered the bright scholar an annual stipend if he would visit the temple regularly and give up his heresies. Spinoza, twenty-three years old, declined the offer. In 1656, one day after Rembrandt was declared bankrupt, the synagogue banned Spinoza: "According to the decision of the Angels and the judgment of the Holy Men we banish, renounce, curse, and damn Baruch de Espinoza, with permission of the Holy God and consent of the congregation." After a long and somber blast on the ram's horn, candles in the temple were extinguished one by one, and the congregation was shrouded in darkness to symbolize that the spiritual life of the one condemned was dead. His fellow Jews were not allowed to talk or correspond with him.

Spinoza lived quietly in Amsterdam with a non-Jewish family, grinding lenses for his livelihood, until the Amsterdam magistrate, perhaps under pressure from the rabbis, banished him from the town. While writing his life's work, *Ethica*, Spinoza anonymously published *Tractatus Theologico-Politicus,* a treatise which was immediately recognized as his. The book was read all over Europe and admired or torn to shreds for such statements as "In a free state everyone should be able to think what he wants and say what he wants. The real purpose of the state is freedom." The regents of Holland, forever fearing an undermining of their position, promptly banned all Spinoza's books.

The philosopher paid no attention. He ground his lenses, studied, and wrote. Evenings he walked through The Hague, dressed in black, a crisp white collar offsetting his long, black curls. Often he had visitors. Scholars from abroad discussed philosophy, and local people came to him with their personal problems. Spinoza would sit in the living room of the good people who lodged him and ask about the Sunday sermon, praising the dominie for his thoughts and reassuring the landlady that she would be blessed if she devoted her life to God.

At the age of forty-five, Baruch Spinoza died of tuberculosis, probably aggravated by the dust from his lenses. Friends published *Ethica* posthumously. Eighty years after Spinoza's death a bookseller in Amsterdam was still fined for selling a copy. Eventually, though, the Dutch authorities approved Spinoza's books, and in more tolerant times he was recognized as a sublime thinker, respected by and influencing men like Goethe and Hegel.

Not of lasting world fame, but certainly outstanding in her own time was Anna Maria Schuurman, who taught herself geometry and astronomy and took language classes at the University of Franeker, where she sat hidden in a cubicle off the lecture room. Women were not admitted to the universities.

In a time when few women were able to read and write, Anna Schuurman asserted, "Woman has the same erect bearing as man, the same ideas, the same love of beauty, honor, truth, the same wish for self-development, the same longing after righteousness, and yet she is to be imprisoned in an empty soul of which the very windows are shuttered."

The "windows" of Anna Schuurman's soul, thanks to her self-study, were wide open. She corresponded with the great in science and literature at home and abroad, even writing in difficult Arabic. She learned Hebrew, Latin, and Greek to better interpret the Scriptures. Gradually she became disenchanted with the dogma of the Calvinist church and at sixty said farewell to the secular life and joined a religious community where all goods were shared and women were equal to men.

The Golden Age was a time of enormous creativity, but the Dutch tire of repeated attention to this long bygone era. The only great Dutch the tourists seem to have heard about are Rembrandt and Vermeer. Vincent van Gogh and Piet Mondrian, however, are more recent artists of commanding greatness. And in the last two decades two Dutch scientists won Nobel prizes—the brothers van Tinbergen: Jan (economy, 1969) and Nicholaas (physiology, 1973).

The Dutch tend to disagree about the relative merits of other recent achievements, and yet few argue about one outstanding cultural monument: the gigantic engineering project in the incessant Dutch struggle with the water—the bridges, dams, locks, and sluices of the Delta Works.

A painting of Saint Elizabeth's flood in 1421.

CHAPTER 3

THE WATERWOLF

THE WATER ROSE slowly against the dike. When it reached
the top, it made a rill and started to flow inland. As the breach
deepened and widened, the water galloped towards the
houses, the church, and the farms in the fields, and engulfed
them all.

"The waterwolf has come again!" the survivors cried.
They repaired the dike, let the water run off, cleaned up the
debris, and went right back to living on their flood-prone
land.

No wonder the Dutch developed a spirit of tenacity and
perseverance.

Not all floods could be turned. Even today, you'll see
Verdronken Land van Saeftinge ("Drowned Land of Saeftinge") on maps of Zeeland. The Saint Felix flood took it in
1530. Southeast of Rotterdam, where the Saint Elizabeth's
flood swallowed sixty-five villages in 1421, stream-logged
Biesbos is a mecca for boaters, anglers, and nature watchers.
The land swept away by the Saint Nicasius flood in the
1200s became the Zuiderzee ("Southern Sea"), a big fist of
the North Sea thrusting deep inland.

When the Romans first saw these areas, now called the
Low Netherlands, they were a maze of rivers, creeks, and
marshes with only an occasional patch of good, firm soil.
Here people lived precariously. Their land flooded when the
rivers overflowed or when the sea broke through the thin row

of coastal dunes. Treacherous though they were, the waterways and the sea were full of fish and carried traders' boats
laden with precious merchandise. The people stayed near the
means of their existence and fought the very water that
provided it for two thousand years. The people won. They
gained 1.8 million acres of land and lost 1.4 million.

At first, they were merely on the defensive. The Romans,
who moved onto the sodden delta between the Rhine, Meuse,
and Scheldt, built dikes along the unruly rivers. Farther
north, the Frisians carried clay in willow baskets to the
mounds where they lived above the tidal sea that flowed in
and out over their land.

"An incredible sea lung is in the north," wrote the Greek
Pytheas about 325 B.C. "Water rises and falls regularly!"
Pliny, a Roman historian, added in A.D. 47, "When the tide
rises, the miserable people are marooned on their mounds
and look like sailors on a ship. When the tide ebbs, they look
like shipwrecks on an island." Since the Mediterranean
knows no tides, Pytheas and Pliny were quite naturally
amazed by the pulsing of the sea.

Should your travels take you to the land of the Frisians, the
present provinces of Friesland and Groningen, visit the hefty
sea dike that protects them from the Wadden Sea. At one
point during the day, you'll look out over the water laced with
whitecaps and see a ferry boat making its way to one of the
Wadden Islands beyond. If you come back six hours later,
water and boats are gone. Hikers walk on rippled sand.

The people took the offensive when they began taking land
from the sea. They let the tides deposit silt against a sea dike
until the silt remained above water at high tide, and then they
diked in the silt. This process took thirty or forty years. The
marine grasses that grew on the reclaimed land fed cattle.
These first polders were known as "onion polders" because
they grew out from the shoreline like the skin of an onion.

Inner dikes gave extra protection. Now you may see a water-turning "watcher dike," backed up by a "sleeper dike." Sometimes a "dreamer dike" forms a third line of defense. In case of emergency, openings in the inner dikes like roads and such are closed off with heavy steel doors or bars slid one on top of another in slots.

In the river delta to the south, extensive diking ceased when the Romans left in the fourth century and was not resumed until the twelfth. At that time the powerful lords of Holland and Zeeland began to use their feudal privileges to have their farmers work for the common good. They not only built dikes to protect the land, but they also drained marshes to make them habitable, built river dams to divert water, and dug canals to channel it. Weary men scooped up thousands upon thousands of cubic feet of clay and sand, which they hauled away in sacks of hide or on sleds. The forebears of the Dutch built their first diked-in polders by hand.

And then, in 1461, a pump operated by wind-driven energy emptied a little lake north of Alkmaar. The windmill, an invention imported from the Middle East, eased the burden of the peasantry. Merchants took over diking from the feudal lords—strictly as a real estate investment. During the Golden Age, when merchants had money to spend, one lake after another was turned to land.

The dike master and his crew built two parallel ring dikes around a lake to contain a ring canal into which windmills on the inner dike pumped the lake water. The surplus water from the canal was channeled into the *boezem*, that complex of waterways where water is stored until it can be cast into the sea via other waterways through a system of sluices. After draining the lake, the windmills stood guard, sometimes for hundreds of years, to pump excess water out of the polder into the boezem. In times of drought, water from the boezem was pumped back into the polder.

"The draining of lakes is one of the most necessary, most profitable, and most holy works in Holland [province]," wrote Jan Leeghwater, a pioneer in seventeenth-century land reclamation. It was necessary because lakes grew bigger as the locals dug up the peat in them to dry and burn, and storm-tossed lakes threatened nearby towns. It was profitable because the new polders were fertile.

One wonders how profitable Jan Leeghwater's know-how was to himself. Leeghwater, whose surname translates into English as "empty water," didn't even own a pair of shoes. When he traveled to counsel the kings and queens of Europe on draining marshes, he first went to his village and borrowed the community pair.

By Leeghwater's time the Dutch had learned a lot about their water housekeeping. Unfortunately, because of the way the republic was set up, they lacked a central authority to enforce laws. Laws were on the books that forbade digging peat in lakes or beyond the sea dikes, where holes filled with water and undermined the dikes, but the Dutch went right on digging. What else was there to burn in woodless regions but peat? Besides, the little piles of salt that were left after burning the sea peat fetched money at the market.

No central agency coordinated projects. If a landowner built a dam to divert water from his land, it flooded someone else's property. If a merchant drained a lake to go into the dairy business, local fishermen lost their livelihood—and not a few pierced brand-new dikes in anger.

Of course, in each *waterschap* ("watership," as in township), the polder board had control over its district's dikes, locks, sluices, and vital waterways, but the six thousand autonomous waterschappen in the republic rarely worked together.

"We cannot pride ourselves on having had an abundance of brotherly feelings," wrote Dr. J. van Veen in his warm and witty book, *Dredge Drain Reclaim: The Art of a Nation*. "The strength of our individuality became our weakness. Feuds often prevented the execution of positive work." He tells about a dike section near Reimerswaal that was in bad repair in 1532. According to the rules of the watership, the lord of Lodijke had to strengthen it, but he was not well disposed towards Reimerswaal. "Oh, let the little harbor drown," said the lord. The feeble dike gave way in a storm and the little harbor drowned. "A little delay, a tiny quarrel," van Veen concludes, "and there goes the property of thousands of hardworking farmers and burghers."

Finally, at the end of the eighteenth century, the Dutch established a full-fledged Ministerie van Waterstaat ("Ministry for the State of the Water"). It took care of—and paid for—the upkeep and construction of dikes, dams, and bridges for the country's growing network of roads, the dredging of harbors and waterways, and the ever-more-costly and ever-bigger land reclamation works.

In the mid-1800s the Ministry of Water drained Lake Haarlem, a project that had been but a dream of Jan Leeghwater years before. He had proposed pumping it dry with 160 windmills. The ministry used only three steam pumps. If you fly into Amsterdam's Schiphol Airport today, your plane will land on what once was Lake Haarlem, the scene of a mighty naval battle in the Eighty Years War!

The Ministry of Water's next big project began in 1919 when it set about taming the troublesome Zuiderzee. The department's water wizards closed off the big fist of the North Sea with a dam between North Holland and Friesland, flushed the sea water from the resulting lake, allowed rivers to bring in fresh water, and, after sixty years of work, pulled four cultivated polders from their hats.

The first step in the Zuiderzee Works was the construction of a 1½-mile dam connecting North Holland and the island of

Wieringen. It took five years to complete because the sea, as if furious at being subjugated, struck it down time and again. Then the engineers and "polder boys,"that tough breed of hip-booted Dutchmen who strangle streams and shut out seas, took the next step. With dredges and cranes they dug up the Zuiderzee clay at one spot and dumped it at another spot to mold a ring dike which stretched from the North Holland shore to Wieringen and the hard-won dam. In six months the lake within the ring dike was pumped dry. A few years later farmers planted potatoes in the country's newest addition, the Wieringermeerpolder ("Lake Wieringen Polder"). Transport barges sailed right up to the farms on canals that had been dug by big machines when the land was still immersed.

In 1927, an army of engineers and polder boys began work from two opposite points on the Afsluitdijk, the twenty-mile closing dam. In spite of machines men still had to pass basalt boulders from hand to hand. Thousands of these rocks were needed to sink the huge, hand-plaited willow mattresses that formed the dam's foundation. Flexible enough to fit the contours of the sea bottom, resilient enough to withstand the scouring tides, the mattresses had to be sunk at the exact moment between low and high tide, or they would be swept by the current and settle in a crumpled heap on the bottom of the North Sea.

As the two sections started to come together with uncanny precision, tension mounted among the crews. The tides would scour harder with the narrowing of the gap. The last loads might not hold. The last load was dumped. It held. The gap was closed! Few people who were in The Netherlands in 1932 will forget the excitement of the radio broadcast. Every boat near the closure whistled and tooted, and a band played the national anthem. In the following decades the country would take five hundred thousand acres of land from the sea.

The old waterwolf could no longer rampage along the Zuiderzee's two hundred miles of coast. Nor would the sea infiltrate the waterways and strew salt in the fields along their banks. The remains of the sea would be renamed Lake IJssel after the main river feeding into it.

At first, the land reclamation seemed to be a mixed blessing as mosquitoes threatened to claim it for themselves. Drivers on the roads near Lake IJssel's shores could hardly see as windshield wipers squashed the pesky insects into a view-obscuring slime. The fishermen living around the former sea raised accusing fingers toward heaven. The scourge was clearly sent by God for tampering with his sea.

Then fishery experts suggested a midnight opening of the dam's sluices that regulate Lake IJssel's water level. Millions of eels swept through in search of freshwater food. The nocturnal fish had been asleep in the mud when the sluices were open during the day. Now they feasted on mosquito larvae and ended the plague.

Some of the fishermen settled for catching eels and freshwater fish instead of herring and anchovy. Others began sailing to distant seas in boats the government helped them buy, using the locks in the closing dam to sail home. A few fisher folk reluctantly gave up their trade and were trained for shore jobs in industries the government encouraged in the former fishing villages.

Relocating or redirecting dislocated fishermen was just half the job of turning sea bottom into land. The government also had to plan for the settlement of the polders. No one could move to a new polder until the state had completed a sewage system, roads, and housing. The delay pointed up a big difference from the settlement of Lake Haarlem Polder a hundred years earlier. At that time the government had leased the land just as it emerged from the water without amenities of any kind. Now settlers for the new polders were also selected carefully for their skills in farming, other trades, and the professions, and they were chosen from different religious groups to balance the population of the new communities. Men who helped build the Northeast Polder, completed in the 1940s, had first choice there. Families who lost their farms during the Zeeland flood of 1953 could take their pick in Oostelijk Flevoland ("Eastern Flevoland") which fell dry in 1957. Townspeople from crowded Amsterdam are now prime candidates for the settlements in Zuidelijk Flevoland ("Southern Flevoland"), parts of which still have the naked, muddy look of land just risen from the sea.

Plans for the newer polders have been modified to suit people's changing tastes and the country's needs. Self-contained small communities close to farms that had seemed ideal in the Northeast Polder were not repeated in those that followed. The communities were too isolated; people preferred to drive to the "mainland" for their movies and beer. Since the post-World War II switch from an agricultural to an industrial economy, the Dutch don't need the farmland that was foreseen on the original blueprints. The use to which the fifth and last polder was to be put was long a matter of national debate. The government even invited popular opinions in a "Help Us Think" campaign. Viable options included an additional airport, an industrial area, and another dormitory town for Rim City Holland. Environmentalists wanted no drainage at all to preserve the habitat of fish and water birds. Late in 1979 a compromise was made: the Markerwaard will be a polder for agricultural use and urban overflow, but smaller than originally planned.

Some tourists who drive over the long sea dikes of the Lake IJssel polders are thrilled by the sight of combines gathering wheat where fishermen once gathered fish in their nets, but others find the new land monotonous. Farms with red-tiled roofs pulled low over their walls like woolen bonnets stand an equal distance apart. Trees line straight roads in military precision, and the sandy public beaches look as artificial as they really are. In the towns everything is neat and orderly and obviously planned with care. Even the ducks in the canals are provided with wicker nesting baskets. Nowhere does a fine old building lean forward from standing for centuries on the shifting Dutch soil.

In the country, there isn't a romantic windmill in sight. Electric pumps now stand guard to pump excess water out of the polders into Lake IJssel, which functions as a boezem and freshwater reservoir. The pumping stations are attractive brick buildings decorated with art inside and named after famous men. The Gemaal Lely in Lake Wieringen Polder honors Dr. Cornelis Lely, who drafted the Zuiderzee Plan. In Eastern Flevoland a *gemaal* ("pumping station") is named after my grandfather, Dr. Hendrikus Colijn, who was prime minister during the years when Lely's plans were implemented at long last. Nearly thirty years went by before they were voted into law.

The Dutch are a cautious race. They do not like to "go over one night's ice," as they say, and they give slow deliberation to matters involving the taxpayers' money. If the Dutch hadn't conferred for so many years about ways to remedy the inadequacy of the sea dikes in the southwest, a catastrophe might have been averted.

On January 31, 1953, flags flew all over The Netherlands in honor of the fifteenth birthday of Crown Princess Beatrix. The flags tore in the wind. Weather forecasters announced increasingly severe northwesterly winds during the night.

On the islands of South Holland and Zeeland the storm knocked out electricity. Men stumbled around in the dark to check on the dikes. Church bells ringing with the short peals that mean alarm brought fear to all who heard them. But many people were asleep. Anguished citizens knocked on doors or threw stones against windows. "Wake up, wake up, our dike is in danger!"

The sea rose high and higher, washing over dikes and smashing them. At Colijnsplaat men put their shoulders to a wall of sandbags in a breach until the water went down and thus saved their village. At Oudekerk, on a branch of the Rhine, a skipper ran his old barge into the potential breaking point and saved the dike.

By daybreak a vast area was under water, and through the breaches more water was gushing in. Families clung to rooftops and were swept away before helicopters could lift them off. In one terror-filled night and day eighteen hundred people lost their lives, tens of thousands of animals drowned, and four hundred thousand acres of land received a lethal soaking of sea water. Seven years of reconditioning were needed before agricultural production reached normal levels again.

Plans for the Delta Works were hurriedly passed into law. The water wizards of the Waterstaat did to the delta what they had done to the Zuiderzee. They closed off four sea arms and shortened the coastline by four hundred miles, thus keeping the battering tides away from the islands' dikes and minimizing salination of the islands' soil. As an additional bonus, the long-isolated islands were linked to the rest of the country by roads on the closing dams. The plan stopped short of land reclamation, however. It called for the water behind the barriers to be left as a boezem for polder drainage, for water reservoirs, and a much-needed recreational area.

Four bodies of water are now closed off: the Meuse near Briel, the Veere Estuary, the Haringvliet, and the Brouwershaven Estuary. The dam over the Eastern Scheldt is still under construction. Meanwhile, this estuary is spanned by the Zeeland Bridge, the longest and one of the most graceful bridges in Europe.

Dam building in The Netherlands has become sophisticated. Radar studies the behavior of waves in the delta estuaries. Radioactive isotopes reveal the hidden movements of sand. During a cold winter in the 1960s, ice floes were colored with aniline red, green, and purple dye to find out how the floes traveled through the labyrinthine delta waterways. As a result of the study the Haringvliet dam was built with sluice doors large enough to let slabs of ice through.

Computers calculate the optimum time to lower the huge concrete caissons that close the gaps in the dams. They now rest on nylon carpets instead of on the hand-plaited willow mattresses that lie at the bottom of so many Dutch dams. In recent years this created a unique national emergency. As willow twigs were less in demand, used only for the repair of the smaller collar pieces at the sides of the dikes, thousands of willows toppled over from the weight of their branches. Brigades of volunteers have been organized to prune willows on weekends. The Dutch wouldn't dream of letting these characteristic sentinels of Dutch polder streams die from lack of care.

All water-turning dikes in the country are raised to delta height, that is, ten meters above NAP ("Normaal Amsterdam Peil"), the normal Amsterdam water level used as a basis for measuring water levels throughout the land. Villages that nestled against the dikes for centuries have to go. But when the Delta Works in the southwest is completed and the thousand miles of river and sea dikes have reached delta height, the chances of another flood are calculated to be 1 in 20,000. After two thousand years it looks as if the Dutch will finally keep the waterwolf at bay.

The U.S. Military Cemetery in Margraten, Limburg. On Memorial Day Dutch schoolchildren decorate the graves of the American soldiers who gave their lives to liberate The Netherlands in World War II.

CHAPTER 4

AN UNDERGROUND WAR

MAY 14, 1940, WAS A BRIGHT, sunny day. Incredulous people, eager for news, crowded the sidewalks of Rotterdam's inner city. The Nazis were occupying Austria, Czechoslavakia, and Poland. Four days earlier German troops had crossed the Dutch border.

From the skies a faint droning noise swelled. German planes, coming in waves, dropped their loads of bombs. The heart of Rotterdam was a furnace of blazing flames and acrid smoke.

Amid the smouldering ruins the streets were deserted except for one man. He saw nothing. He heard nothing. He stood there, clenching his fists, repeating over and over again, "I won't take it, I won't take it."

The next day the Dutch army capitulated. An agonized Queen Wilhelmina left for London with key figures of her government to avoid falling in enemy hands. There she joined other wartime governments in exile. Hitler installed a new head of state, Dr. Arthur Seyss-Inquart, an ardent Nazi.

For five long years Dutch officials stayed at their posts and took orders from Seyss in obedience to a higher authority— their prewar government. In case of foreign invasion they had been instructed to "effectuate the administration as well as possible in the interest of the population."

How was this to be interpreted? the officials asked themselves. When the Germans ordered mayors to requisition cars, radios, gold, tin, copper, and even bronze church bells, should the mayors cooperate? If they did not, they would surely be dismissed and replaced by pro-Nazi NSB-ers, members of the Nationaal Socialistische Bond ("the National Socialist League"). The officials complied.

In November 1940 the Germans decreed that all Jews be removed from government posts, schools, and universities. Again Dutch officials complied, except for a few who resigned. "As a Christian I cannot put myself over someone of another race," said one. Three weeks later the Germans put him in prison.

Dutch manufacturers were also in a quandary. The Germans ordered production increases to aid the German war effort. Should the manufacturers go along or refuse? If they did, their factories would surely be taken over by Germans and Dutch workers laid off. The factories turning out war materiel "suddenly" developed technical problems, and orders were slowly filled.

In 1943 fourteen thousand Dutch university students were told they could not continue their studies unless they signed a paper declaring, "I shall refrain from any act against the German Reich and the German Army." Was it the students' duty to sign this loyalty oath so that they could continue classes and provide a newly liberated nation with a fresh crop of university graduates? Eighty-six percent of the students did not sign. Universities closed.

Many Dutch were spared such moral dilemmas, but the enemy presence was felt by all. Every Dutch person over the age of fifteen had to carry an identity card called a *persoons-bewijs (pb)* with a photo and fingerprint and show this card to any German who asked for it. Every Dutch organization was dissolved. The Nazis set up physicians' and lawyers' guilds, an artists' cultural chamber, and youth and labor corps, but few Dutch joined unless they had to.

The churches were left alone, however. Priests and dominies prayed openly for the return of Wilhelmina long after street signs with her name had been removed and her ancestors were censored out of history textbooks.

Patriotic Dutch categorized their wartime population in two groups: collaborators and everyone else. The former were NSB-ers, Nazi sympathizers and opportunists who spied for the Germans, volunteered for German jobs, and accepted German favors. While the rest of the population walked or rattled along on old bicycles, collaborators drove cars. The loyal Dutch called them "wrong." "Right" were those who were either passively "not wrong" or actively working in the resistance.

Brave men, women, and teenagers nursed downed Allied fliers and stashed away arms air-dropped by the Allies. They established secret radio contacts with the exiled London government and helped recruits get out of their hermetically sealed country to join Allied forces abroad. They sabotaged German military installations.

The resistance also hid "underdivers"—those who were being sought by German police. Dutch Jews were the first to "dive under." At first Jewish people were banished from public life and then their shops were confiscated. They were forced to wear the yellow star of David, and later they were barred from using parks, public transportation, and telephones. Then they were evicted from their homes and shipped by train to a transit camp in Drenthe from which cattle cars took them to unknown destinations. As the world now knows, extermination camps in Germany and Poland awaited them.

Those who avoided the roundups were afraid to go out and be recognized as Jews. They lived, sometimes for years, in a small space with many others. Tempers exploded about the noisy way David blew his nose or Selma repeated, "Well, I never!" Gentle Anne Frank mentions in her haunting diary how the van Daans bickered with her parents.

What to do with underdivers who died? After dark, one resistance worker put a dead woman in a wheelchair and went to an Amsterdam canal. "In peacetime I would have walked arm in arm with a boyfriend," she wrote after the war. "Now through a mist of tears I saw a little Jewish grandmother disappear in the dark water." The resistance worker was eighteen.

Not all Jews found refuge, or wished to dive under. Some of them did not want to be separated as a family—often a must—or to endanger the lives of those who were willing to harbor them. Others did not believe that God would permit their total destruction. Of the twenty-two thousand Dutch Jews who went into hiding, an estimated one-third were betrayed, usually by collaborators lured into collecting a small German bounty for each Jew denounced.

New Nazi ordinances jarred the nation. Dutch men between the ages of eighteen and forty had to work in Germany. The annual quota was one hundred thousand the first year and more than one hundred fifty thousand in later years, when the age limit was upped to sixty. Those who were unwilling to work in German war industries did not report to the recruiting stations and dived under. So did a growing number of resistance workers on German blacklists and Dutch officials who no longer felt that cooperating with the enemy was in the best interest of the population.

By the summer of 1944, more than three hundred thousand people were hiding from the Nazis, usually in other people's homes—behind doors concealed by a china cabinet or a bookcase, in a cluttered attic, in a musty cellar, or in a backyard chicken coop. In rural areas, when no snooping Germans were about, underdivers helped with farm work. In some North Holland villages 10 percent of the population were there illegally and could depend on the watchful eyes and the help of local lads. If an infrequent German patrol asked where they might find Farmer Jansen (known to all in the village as sheltering several underdivers), a boy might say, "Way down that road to the right," and race towards the left to warn Jansen. His guests dashed to a wheatbin or plunged into a canal and stood up to their shoulders in the water with their heads hidden in the rushes until the coast was clear.

In rural areas hosts shared home-grown food with their illegal visitors and lessened the worries of the Landelijke Organisatie voor Hulp aan Onderduikers ("National Organization for Help to Underdivers," abbreviated LO). Many underdivers could not work for their food nor did they have money to pay for it.

The resistance created the National Support Fund, which borrowed money from "good" banks and charged the absentee Dutch government. Women on bicycles carried as much as a million guilders cash on their persons, often on trips of a hundred miles a day, to LO district centers where the money was distributed so underdivers could eat.

To provide fugitives with desperately needed food coupons for storebought rations, masked resistance men known as KP-ers raided food coupon distribution centers. The KP-ers were frequently aided by Dutch office workers who "just forgot" to lock the door the night before a raid.

The Nazis gave short shrift to those who were caught. "We always worried that someone might be absent at our weekly meeting," a former KP-er later recalled. "One day Bertus told us he had good news. After fourteen years his wife was pregnant. But next week Bertus was missing."

Another resourceful resistance group falsified pbs for underdivers and other "illegals" who might be halted in the street by the German police. Each pb took hours to make and then it had to go through a press six times. The counterfeiters of the resistance became so well organized that a worker could order a certain kind of type, town seal, and facsimile of a German signature by number from a central catalog.

As the Germans realized they were losing the war, they stepped up reprisals. When the Dutch underground set a regional Population Register office afire to burn telltale copies of the pbs, the Nazis shot a number of imprisoned illegals without trial. After the underground killed a key German who was suspected of carrying a list of underdive addresses, the Nazis transported all the men in one village to a German concentration camp. Such terror tactics only made the people more angry. The resistance gained supporters.

"The Germans make lead to make bullets and kill; the illegal printers melt lead to make birds that fly out with the voice of the people," one resistance worker wrote. As many as sixty illegal newspapers were printed on small hidden presses or on "German presses" at night and on weekends when the regular printers were at home. Some papers achieved a circulation as high as a hundred thousand. There was even one in Braille for the blind. When the men and women who worked on the illegal newspapers were discovered, they were shot by German firing squads, and yet the presses kept on rolling. The Dutch had to learn the truth about Allied gains.

England's courageous and ultimately victorious stand in the Battle of Britain, the entry of the United States into the war, and the huge German losses in Russia were reported in optimistic terms. Each time it seemed to the shackled Dutch that they would soon be freed.

On D day in June 1944 they looked at the map and counted the days it should take Allied troops to get from the Normandy coast to The Netherlands. Ignoring the logistics of troop movements and the possibility that the Germans might resist the Allied march north, the Dutch cheered. Clearly, the nightmare would be over soon.

On August 24, Paris surrendered to the Allies. On September 3, Brussels fell. The exiled government in London broadcast to the Dutch huddled around their forbidden radios: "The liberation is at your door, tune in for instructions." On September 4, Antwerp, only a few miles from the Dutch border, was liberated. On September 5 people in The Hague and Rotterdam were telling each other that the Allies were coming.

No one wanted to miss their arrival. Streets were crowded. Children stood on the sidewalks with little paper British flags.

A youth club which the Germans had dissolved in 1940 circulated its liberation issue in thousands of copies. An illegal paper printed an issue with names of its editors on the masthead for the first time. Fortunately, that paper was not circulated.

Germans drove in panic to Germany while the NSB-ers packed their bags and nervously wondered where they should go.

No liberators came on that "Mad Tuesday," nor the day after, nor the next.

On September 17 the Dutch voice from London said, "Here is an important message from the Dutch government. . . . After consultation with the Allied Command, the government deems the moment has come to give instructions for a general strike of the railroad workers in order to hinder enemy transport and troop concentrations." Some thirty thousand Dutch railroad workers risked the death sentence to go on strike and dived under. They thought they would be hiding for only the few weeks that the war would continue. Little could the strikers foresee that the railroad strike would last nearly eight months.

It was not until the end of 1944 that the southern Netherlands fell into Allied hands, after fierce fighting between the Allied and German armies in the Dutch provinces of Zeeland, North Brabant, and Limburg. Civilians who could not be evacuated were caught between air attacks and gunfire and lived in cellars or dugouts in the woods. Just as the Dutch had done in the Eighty Years War, the Allies flooded land to flush out the enemy. They bombed breaches in the sea dikes of Walcheren and covered the island with water. Zeelanders drowned. They had not believed the paper warnings fluttering down from Allied planes.

A Dutch military command under the leadership of Prince Bernhard, husband of the crown princess Juliana, took control of the freed south. The north remained occupied. When the Allies lost the battle of the bridgeheads at Arnhem, The Netherlands was sliced in two. Cut off from the coal mines in Limburg, the north had no fuel to heat homes, to operate gas factories, and to generate electricity.

The Nazis, however, put German personnel on some of the idle trains and brought in coal from Germany so that they could use the telephone, have electricity, and be assured that the polder pumps were operating. A flooded land would thwart Germany's military plans. Furious about the absence of regular Dutch train service, the Germans were not about to use the few German-operated trains to transport food for the Dutch from the rural parts of The Netherlands to the urban west. Here people went hungry. When pleas to the German authorities finally resulted in permission to transport food on the waterways, they were covered with ice.

By January 1945 the daily ration in the west had shrunk to five hundred calories. After lengthy negotiations with the Germans, the Dutch received coal for central kitchens. Every day long lines of householders waited with buckets to collect a pint of thin soup per family member. For many this soup was the only hot meal of the day—or whatever was left of "hot" by the time the people trudged home.

Without gas and electricity, home cooking was often impossible unless wood was found. Legions of Dutch fanned out over the parks and chopped down trees, dug up ties from the tracks of streetcars that were no longer running, and stripped the sadly still homes of the deported Jews or dismantled their own. A wooden balcony was fine for making a fire around which freezing children could sit; a closet door was bartered on the black market for bread, sugar, or tulip bulbs, which the Dutch now ate.

Only women, children, and elderly men were out in the streets. Able-bodied men had long been in hiding to escape Nazi roundups for workers. If conscripted, Dutchmen had to help strengthen German fortifications in The Netherlands.

Those who could show their faces without fear of arrest went from town to farms in search of food. They walked through mud and roads half submerged in water. Some carried gold and jewelry in their pockets or pushed a baby buggy filled with linens. Money was useless since the farmers were interested only in bartering their potatoes and their peas. Besides, many of the starving people did not have cash. Some did not even have barter goods but hoped the farmer would say, "Pay me later," or "Here, young lady, have this," and some farmers did. Country families gave the "hunger trekkers" a square meal as they arrived exhausted from their long journeys and bedded them down on the living room floor.

Fifteen thousand people died that winter from hunger and cold.

In London, Wilhelmina received the somber news, "For 3.5 million people in the western Netherlands only three weeks of rations are left. After that there'll be nothing."

The end came just in time. Allied planes dropped bags of flour, dried meat, potato powder, and dried vegetables. Long lines of military trucks that had been waiting below the rivers arrived with additional food.

On May 5, 1945—eleven months after D day—all of The Netherlands was free.

Dutch flags flew again from houses and official buildings. The national anthem was heard, and many people wept.

All over the polder land the arms of windmills were set in their "celebration" position—the top arm pointing at five minutes past twelve. One farmer decorated his barn with brightly colored parachutes.

Children rode on British and Canadian tanks. Adults were acutely aware of how reassuring it was to see men in uniform whom they need not fear. The soldiers passed out real cigarettes, the first the Dutch had seen in several years.

In the evening, lights shone from the houses and people milled in the streets. Five years of a rigidly enforced blackout and curfew were over.

The royal family returned. Citizens were delighted to see Juliana's little girls, Beatrix and Irene, and baby Margriet, born in Canada where Juliana spent her exile.

Wilhelmina toured the country. At first, her admirers had been shocked when she left in 1940 and had torn her portrait off the wall. Gradually realizing that leaving had been the only plausible thing for her to do, they had put the queen back in their hearts and eagerly listened to her words of encouragement and consolation over Radio Oranje. And now she was here in person, and they whooped "Long Live Wilhelmina!" Even Dutch antimonarchists cheered. This short, stocky, 64-year-old woman was a symbol of Dutch pluck and unity.

The country had to be "purified" of those who had been "wrong." Traitors were tried before special courts and received prison terms. Thirty-seven were shot for high treason. The circumstances of the war demanded these sentences even though capital punishment had been abolished in The Netherlands since 1870.

The Dutch talked a lot among themselves about the purification. What was "right" during the occupation and what was "wrong?" Where ended the officials' service to the country as outlined in the prewar government directives, and where did help to the Germans begin?

Wartime attitudes are still the subject of often-heated discussions. You may read in a Dutch paper that someone is bypassed for a position because he was "wrong" in the war. Or someone who is suspected of having been "wrong" but who never had a trial is now brought before a civil court.

Of the 140,000 Jews in The Netherlands, more than 100,000 did not come back. Another 140,000 Dutch died in the resistance, in German reprisal killings, in concentration camps, in air raids, in the "hunger winter," and on the seas where Dutch navy and merchant ships were hit by torpedoes and blown up with mines.

May 4 was set aside for national mourning, and each year on that day flowers are laid at war memorials. In Winterswijk stands a stone statue of a woman with a sheep—a tribute to one housewife who was sent to a concentration camp for sheltering underdivers and to all the other Dutch women who laid their lives on the line—and lost them—for the same cause. In the Oosterbegraafplaats ("Eastern Cemetery") in Amsterdam, the flat, broken mirrors of the Auschwitz Monument distort the trees and the clouds, just as the Holocaust forever distorted the lives of survivors. A bronze statue of a sturdy dock worker on the town's Jonas Daniel Meyerplein commemorates the two-day strike of February 1941 when Amsterdam streetcar conductors, shopkeepers, and longshoremen stopped work to protest the first Nazi roundup of Jews, and several protestors were executed.

Events of the war are documented in the Airborne Museum in Oosterbeek, Gelderland; the National War and Resistance Museum in Overloon, North Brabant; and in the Anne Frank House in Amsterdam. Each year millions of visitors climb the narrow stairs of this house on the Prinsengracht, walk through the door hidden behind a bookcase, and stand in awe in the small attic rooms where the Frank family lived behind blackout curtains for more than two years. A photo of Deanne Durbin which Anne cut from a magazine still hangs on a wall.

On the American Memorial Day Dutch children with serious faces lay flowers at the U.S. Military Cemetery in Margraten. Here lie eight thousand men who gave their lives for the liberation of the southern Netherlands. On the stark white marble crosses are the names of eighty pairs of brothers.

The older Dutch will never forget the American sacrifice, just as they will never forget the U.S. Marshall Aid which helped the country pull itself up by its bootstraps. The devastated bridges and roads were repaired. Trains rolled again. Rotterdam received a new core and a shopping center with pedestrian malls that for years has been a showpiece of sensible urban planning.

New homes were hastily put up to meet a gigantic housing shortage. During the war no houses were built, and many were destroyed. Among the Dutch who needed homes were thousands of families who returned from the Dutch East Indies, before and after these colonies became the independent Republic of Indonesia in 1949. Most of the repatriates had lost all their earthly possessions in the early days of Japanese occupation of the Indies, and some had spent as long as three and a half years in concentration camps. What they needed most of all was a decent roof over their head again and a chance to build a new life. Where to find the roofs? Large-scale emigration encouraged by government-paid ship fares to Canada, the United States, Australia, New Zealand, and South Africa partially offset the housing shortage, but for years Dutch newlyweds had to move in with in-laws and total strangers were crowded together on one floor and shared a kitchen and bath.

To restore their shattered finances, the Dutch switched from an agricultural to an industrial economy and they built up their export trade. At the mouth of the Rhine rose a new port for Rotterdam, which is now the largest in the world. The Netherlands joined Belgium and Luxembourg in the Benelux economic partnership and became a member of the European Coal and Steel Community and the Common Market. By the 1960s business was booming. To fill places in industry, the Dutch imported Turkish, Yugoslav, and Moroccan guest workers, who aggravated the housing shortage. Now housing is plentiful, but not all houses are in the right place or of the right kind. Ten percent of Dutch homes still do not have a shower or a bath.

The living standard has never been so high. Half of all Dutch homes are owner-occupied. One out of every four Dutch citizens owns a car. Many own a boat, a trailer home, or a second house in the country. Everyone has enough food to eat and fuel to keep warm. The Dutch have come a long way since the occupation, when children searched for slivers of coal in a train yard so that a sick sister could have a hot cup of soup, when enemy soldiers kicked in doors and shouted, "Everyone, outside!"

The highest advisory government body is the Council of State. This member uses a bicycle for daily transportation as do two million other Dutch men, women, and children.

CHAPTER 5

PILLARS AND POLITICS

THE NUMBER OF political parties in The Netherlands is staggering. In recent parliamentary elections, twenty-five of them tried to lure Dutch voters to their particular cause. With each election more new parties are founded by people with an ax to grind. One of the latest is one with a name that has appeal to many tax-paying citizens, Dutch or not—the Society Against Bureaucratic Arbitrariness.

The proliferation of parties is typical of a society in which people tend to mix only with those who have the same outlook on life. The divisions grew gradually with the development of political parties at the end of the last century. Religious denominations formed their own political groups and eventually established their own schools, unions, newspapers, hospitals, and funeral societies. To Dutch social scientists, they resembled *zuilen* ("pillars") which, although they stood apart, supported the roof of Dutch society.

Until World War II the zuilen were rather rigid. From infancy through retirement many Dutch learned, worked, and played only with those in their own *zuil*. During the occupation a great deal was written in illegal newspapers about the need to do away with these divisive zuilen. And indeed, after the war, greater tolerance seemed to herald their end.

Intermarriage between the faiths ceased to cause irreparable family rifts. In 1976, the Catholic and Socialist workers' unions merged. A year later, Catholic and Protestant politicians overcome a mutual distrust that dated from the Eighty Years War and formed one party. The two largest Protestant parties and the one big Catholic party became the Christian Democratic Appeal.

Although cracked and less rigid, the zuilen still stand, supported by their own broadcasting stations and schools. Small political parties take their stand on a particular religious dogma and even a specific article of creed.

Eleven parties are now represented in the First and Second Chambers of the States-General, the Dutch parliament. Eleven different viewpoints have to be considered every time a bill is introduced in the Second Chamber! This 150-member legislative body, elected by direct national vote, fulfills the same function as the U.S. House of Representatives and the Canadian House of Commons. The 75-member First Chamber, elected by the provincial legislatures, is comparable to the senates in Washington, D.C., and Ottawa.

The eleven parties in parliament run the gamut of Dutch political thinking from the traditional "outlook on life" parties to new parties with new concepts like the Democrats of 1966, who advocate that the prime minister be elected rather than appointed, which they feel would end the often bizarre system of cabinet formations.

The cabinet, assisted by the queen, represents the executive branch of the nation's government.

After the election of Second Chamber representatives, formation of a new cabinet begins when the queen appoints a cabinet *formateur*. She is guided in her choice by members of the Council of State, the presidents of the two chambers, and chamber leaders of all the parties.

The formateur consults with leaders of the large parties in the Second Chamber about a four-year program that will please enough parties so that he can count on majority support. No one party *ever* has a majority!

If the formateur cannot find enough support for his program, the queen appoints an *informateur*, a mediator who helps in the negotiations. If that doesn't bring results, the queen appoints a new formateur and the wheeling and dealing starts all over again.

When a formateur finally has a majority support for a program, he forms a cabinet with members of the coalition parties and usually becomes prime minister.

The fifteen ministerial posts have to be divided in exact proportion to the seats that the coalition parties occupy in the Second Chamber. For example, if the Socialists have half of the coalition seats, they must have half of the ministerial posts. Distribution of cabinet seats tends to add to the length of a cabinet formation. In 1977 the whole process took a record 206 days!

While all the "rope pulling" goes on, the lame duck government cannot introduce important bills. Meanwhile, the Dutch read their newspapers and watch their TV and wonder what sort of cabinet will surface from all the palavers. They expect a coalition with a broad base that represents large parties but even this is far from certain. In 1977 the Socialists became the largest party in the Second Chamber, and everyone assumed that a coalition cabinet would include them. When the queen swore in the new cabinet, however, the Socialists were not represented. The country's largest party wasn't even in the government! None of the several formateurs had succeeded in dividing the ministerial posts in such a way that the Socialists wanted to be in the new cabinet.

It's possible that a cabinet, once it has exercised its executive functions for a while, loses support of the parties that endorsed the cabinet's program at formation time. Then the cabinet "falls," or "steps down." The queen appoints a new cabinet formateur, and the long process of a cabinet formation starts all over again. Twice since World War II none of the formateurs appointed by the queen were able to design a program that pleased a majority in the Second Chamber. The Chamber was dissolved before its four-year term was up, and there were new Second Chamber elections.

Fortunately, in the ever-shifting political scene, one stable figure remains: the monarch. In 1948, Juliana succeeded her mother, Queen Wilhelmina. After a thirty-two year reign, Queen Juliana announced that she would abdicate in favor of Crown Princess Beatrix. Mother and daughter exchanged titles—as Beatrix became queen, her mother became a princess again—on April 30, 1980, Juliana's seventy-first birthday. The new queen, born in 1938, is married to Prince Claus von Amsberg, and their eldest son, Prince Willem-Alexander, born in 1967, is first in line to inherit the Dutch throne. If he succeeds, he will be the first Dutch king since the death of William III in 1880.

The queen does not belong to any of the parties and is "inviolable" in the sense that she is not responsible to parliament as the ministers are. She has virtually no political power.

Among the queen's other tasks are the opening of the new session of the States-General and the appointing of mayors of the country's eight hundred municipalities and the *commissarissen der koningin* ("commissaries of the queen"), who preside over the councils in each of the eleven provinces. (More will emerge if an administrative overhaul creates "mini-provinces.") The members of the provincial councils, as well as those of the municipal councils, are elected.

Although it is too soon to assess national feelings toward the new monarch, it is clear that the Dutch are fond of her predecessor. Juliana is a warm, practical woman who fit right into a democracy. She did away with the title "Your Majesty"; subjects simply called her "*Mevrouw*" ("Mrs."), and they no longer curtseyed nor left the room backwards in the royal presence. Often calling on the sick in hospitals, listening to complaints of ill-housed citizens, and urging reforms, she earned the title "Our Country's No. 1 Social Worker."

The Dutch also revere their monarch as the representative of a historical tradition that goes back four hundred years to Prince William of Orange, who started the revolt against Spain which led to Dutch independence and the emancipation of the Protestants. To staunch Dutch Calvinists "God, The Netherlands, and Orange" are one.

Later princes of Orange held positions of power in the Dutch republic and—in a more or less remarkable fashion— continued the first William's role of benign benefactor to the people. When the republic became a monarchy in 1815, an Orange prince became King William I followed by William II and III, and the Orange women, Wilhelmina, Juliana, and Beatrix.

Some Dutch, however, want to abolish the monarchy. They see it as an archaic and costly institution which is supported by taxpayers' stipends even though the royal family has considerable wealth. At its 1977 congress the Socialist party voted for a republic by a close margin.

For many more Dutch than ever before, it's good living in The Netherlands, and that is due, in part, to the benefits of a social welfare state.

Medical care is complete and lasting. Generous provisions exist for those who do not have work or cannot work because of illness or disability. In keeping with the current trend of encouraging them to live among the nonhandicapped, handicapped persons may have their homes adapted at state expense, or they may be offered specially adapted units in new housing projects at state-controlled rents.

Citizens over sixty-five receive more generous benefits than in most other countries. When necessary, the state pays the costs for living in a senior citizens home which offers independent living units for singles or couples and meals and partial care in such units, as well as complete nursing care in a hospital or convalescent home.

Retired people also receive 6 percent of their annual state pension as vacation pay just as all workers receive 7 percent of their wages or salary to spend on vacation, for which they have an annual minimum of twenty days.

The Netherlands can be a paradise for struggling artists who are unable to sell their work since they may qualify for an annual stipend to cover their living expenses while they pursue their art. Many of the sculptures, paintings, and appliqué hangings seen in public places were done by subsidized artists who have turned their work in to the state.

Subsidies are also available for such projects as publishing an esoteric book about baroque pipe organs or composing a hypermodern opera. The owner of an old house on the National Monument list may receive a subsidy to have the exterior restored and the interior modernized with central heating and a bathroom. The owner of just any old house may qualify for a subsidy for improvements as long as the building is structurally sound. In Amsterdam row upon row of sturdy houses built in the late 1800s fall into the latter category.

The possibilities of state subsidies are so many that the Dutch have coined a word for the person who knows the way through the bureaucratic maze to find the right subsidy: he or she is a "subsidiologist."

Vadertje Staat ("dear Father State") also extends his care to foreign residents. Moslem guest workers may receive financial help for converting a building into a mosque, and gypsies receive a subsidy for new wagons. The state also imports language teachers so that little Tunisians and Moroccans can learn to read and write in their native tongue. South Moluccans are eligible for the state's low-income housing. These ex-colonial soldiers and their families settled in The Netherlands in the late 1950s when against their wishes, the South Moluccan islands became part of the Indonesian Republic. (Young South Moluccan terrorists made international headlines in 1977 when they seized a train and kept schoolchildren hostage to draw attention to their demands for an independent South Moluccan republic.)

Naturally, all these benefits and subsidies cost the Dutch government huge sums of money, and the welfare state does have its critics. Dutch grumble that taxes are exorbitant. People tell each other tales of flagrant abuses of the social benefits. Owners of small businesses complain that they have to pay so many social premiums for their employees, they cannot afford to hire additional workers. Prophets of economic doom predict that the state is heading towards bankruptcy: more money is pouring out of the treasury than is coming in.

Even so, protests against the welfare state do not usually rise above a murmur. The Dutch are more vocal about the many political parties in parliament which hinder the smooth workings of government. Most likely those small parties that have only one or two representatives in parliament will soon disappear. The Dutch call them "outboard motors," because they do not steer the ship of state and yet their votes help to keep it afloat.

The Dutch parties exist because of the Dutch philosophy that each citizen is entitled to his or her opinion, and each opinion must be heard.

Who will say otherwise?

Ice on ponds and canals means a vacation of up to three days a year for schoolchildren.

CHAPTER 6

SCHOOL DAYS

THE DUTCH *are* persevering. Within the Protestant and the
Catholic zuilen, they were so determined to get schools
tailored to their own religions that three generations fought a
school battle for a change in the constitution. In 1917 the
amendment came about. Since that time the national government has subsidized any school parents ask for, provided
enough pupils attend.

As a result, 70 percent of all Dutch elementary school
pupils and 60 percent of secondary school students go to a
bijzonder school. *Bijzonder* means "special" and is used in
an educational context for schools that are administered by a
nongovernmental school board instead of the municipality
in which they are located. Schools abound for every religious interest, and there are a few "neutral " bijzonder
schools as well. "Dear Father State" pays for them all. If the
nearest bijzonder school happens to be in another town, the
state reimburses parents for their children's transportation
and lodging during the week.

In the denominational schools, the days usually begin with
prayers. Catechism and biblical history are included as
regular subjects, but the academic curriculum is the same as
in any other school. The Ministry of Education and Science
sets one basic national program.

No Dutch person claims that the bijzonder schools are
practical. In one small village a Protestant school, a Roman

Catholic school, and a neutral governmental school are within a block of one another, and each is one-third filled! The bijzonder schools add mightily to the cost of Dutch education, which in 1977 took 21 percent of the national budget. The Dutch fought long and hard, however, for the constitutional right to have the schools they wanted, and they are not likely to give them up.

When little Jan and Marie begin school at age six, they go to a bijzonder or public "basis school." Probably they have already attended an optional kindergarten for one to three years. In the basis school they learn the three Rs in much the same way as children do the world over. But after six years they must choose from a variety of secondary schools.

Unlike Americans, who commonly offer general education, vocational training, and a college preparatory program in the same high school, the Dutch have specific schools for specific careers. For example, if three pupils leaving the basis school think they want to become respectively a bookkeeper, plumber, and physicist, they go to three different secondary schools. Some secondary schools grant diplomas, which are vital to getting a job in The Netherlands, while others are stepping-stones to the university or schools of higher vocational training such as teachers colleges, art academies, and nursing schools.

Deciding on one's future career at age twelve or thirteen is a serious matter. In the past this was even more serious because students did not have a chance to change their mind once they had selected a secondary school. Moreover, their choice was often determined by social class and sex. A workingman's son most likely went to a vocational school while his daughter learned to sew and cook in a domestic science school. Upper-class boys went in for the professions.

The inequalities of the system were obvious, and after World War II lawmakers worked for years to make sweeping changes. The popularly called "Mammoth Law" went into effect in 1968.

Now students ready for secondary school are tested for the school which is appropriate for them regardless of their social background. After their first year, called a "bridge class," students can change types of schools if they want to change direction. A student can step sideways or stop at low, middle, or high achievement levels. No one, however, may leave school before age seventeen.

During the last year of required schooling, a student may do part-time work, begin an apprenticeship, or attend a "formation institute." Formation institutes offer young people a chance to study themselves and their role in a changing society. The courses range from motivational programs, which help teenagers find a direction, to classes that deal with family, leisure time, and politics. "The less one knows of all kinds of things, the bigger the chance that others will decide what will happen," warns a government pamphlet dealing with the need for this type of continuing education.

One foreign language is now compulsory in most high schools, and most students choose English so that they can communicate not only with English-speaking people, but also with Swiss, Swedes, and Spaniards who also learn English as their second language. "Expression courses" like singing and dance enliven curricula once dry with factual learning, and physical education is offered more than just once a week.

Schools have eased their demands. Subjects that once were compulsory are now electives. The *gymnasium*, one of several schools that lead to the university, allows students to use a dictionary for the final Latin exams. Before 1968, exam takers had to know every Latin word in a text lifted from Vergil or Tacitus.

Although fewer secondary school students repeat classes

because of failing grades, Americans may still find the odds staggering: in 1976 a four-year study of thirty-six thousand students in university preparatory schools showed that 40 percent had repeated a class.

In spite of their often heavy demands, these schools draw many more students than ever before. As a result, the number of university students in 1978 was six times larger than right after World War II. One-quarter of the new bumper crop were women—a jump from 1945. That year, only 3,245 of the 21,791 students admitted to the university system were women.

The Netherlands has eight universities, all of which are state subsidized: Leiden (1575), Groningen (1614), Utrecht (1636), the Municipal University of Amsterdam (1877), the Protestant Free University of Amsterdam (1880), the Roman Catholic University of Nijmegen (1923), the Erasmus University of Rotterdam (1973), and the University of Maastricht (1976). In addition, five specialized colleges have university status so that they may confer Ph.D. degrees.

A university education is so sought after that enrollment has been limited since 1972. By 1978 eleven disciplines required otherwise qualified applicants to draw for a place. A computer impersonally performed the lottery, and good grades improved a student's chances. In eight disciplines, all applicants were placed, although some had to settle for a university they did not select. Since all Dutch universities have equal prestige, few students found this upsetting. Only medicine, dentistry, and veterinary medicine could not accommodate all applicants. Those for whom the computer drew the wrong number settled for a second choice, switched to a school of higher vocational training, or decided to forgo further education and look for work.

Classes are always connected with the field of study the student has decided upon. In some of the five- to seven-year academic courses, all subjects are rigidly set from beginning to end. In others, students may take some electives. Unlike their American counterparts, Dutch students do not have the opportunity to take choral singing or golf—and earn units of credit at that! They simply grind through the prescribed courses and take periodic exams, after which they are informed by mail of passing or failing grades. Studying at home for a summer to make up an exam in the fall has ruined many a three-month university vacation.

At the end of the academic course, the student earns the title of *doctorandus* (Drs.), which signifies a person who has taken the doctoral exam but has not been promoted to doctor. A law graduate becomes *meester* (Mr.), a church minister a *dominee* (Ds), and a graduate from a technical college an *ingenieur* (Ir.). The Dutch use the abbreviations in correspondence and on business cards.

The ambitious degree-holder may write a thesis to earn the title of doctor and its corresponding abbreviation, Dr. This is officially bestowed during a public promotion to which friends and relatives are invited. But first the candidate has to defend his or her thesis in a ceremony which follows a tradition that is centuries old.

A black-gowned university functionary topped with a beret solemnly enters the hall and taps a silver staff on the floor to announce that the ritual has begun. Directly following him are the five or so "opponents," some of whom are professors invited from other universities. They, too, wear black gowns and jaunty velvet berets.

In the center of the room stands the candidate, wearing a business suit or a dressy dress. Not so long ago, most candidates were male, and the only permissible costume was a morning coat and its formal accessories.

The candidate is flanked by one or two friends, known as *paranimfen* (literally, "bridal attendants"). They may have taken him or her on a nerve-soothing beach walk in the morning, and will arrange for a reception or party when the test is over.

After preliminaries the opponents—seated behind a long table, and having duly read the thesis beforehand—start firing questions at the candidate. Everyone, most of all the "victim," heaves a sigh of relief when the functionary returns, taps the silver staff again and announces in Latin that the hour is up. The candidate breaks off in mid-sentence, and the opponents file out of the hall. Just as in court, they return with a verdict. Since the thesis has already been thoroughly discussed with a "promoter" professor and approved by a faculty committee, the promotion is rarely denied.

The financial arrangements at Dutch universities are all a student could hope for. Anyone whose parents cannot help may obtain a government scholarship and an interest-free loan. In 1978/1979 the combined maximum was about $4400, which most students found sufficient to cover tuition ($250 for the first five years and $40 thereafter), books, and living expenses.

A radical group of Dutch students would like the government to go one step further and *pay* all students for going to school. They would also prefer not to have to attend classes and not to study for more than forty hours a week.

Meanwhile, the people in Academia are worried that the quality of university education will go down. Another gigantic school plan is up for discussion that will affect the entire educational sector, including the universities. University courses could be shortened to four years of practical, job-oriented training. Those who want the academic fluff could then continue for another two or three years.

The urgency of the proposals put forth changes with each new minister of education, but they promise sweeping changes. There's talk of having schools where pupils choose what they want to learn and have complete freedom of movement. The now optional kindergarten may be fused with elementary school, and Dutch children would begin school at age four or even younger. They would stay in elementary school for eight years even though the traditional school "years" might be eliminated in favor of competence levels. This would be helpful to slow learners and children loosely grouped together as "culturally handicapped." Among them are children of parents who have had only six years of schooling and children of cultural minorities like Moluccans, and Surinamers, and Mediterranean guest workers who do not speak Dutch at home. No boy or girl would have to repeat a class because of poor grades— a happy situation which is proposed for all educational levels.

Secondary education would be revamped again. Instead of the specialized schools created by the Mammoth Law, there would be only one four-year middle school with separate streams, just like the American high school. A three-year school for sixteen-to nineteen-year-olds might form a bridge between secondary and tertiary education. It would have one academic and two vocational streams.

There's more to the new plans, like upping the age for leaving school to eighteen and having the government pay for all education up to that age. In a concept similar to the "mainstreaming" now being done in the United States, students with mental and physical handicaps would attend regular schools.

Some of the plans may be implemented soon, but others are likely to be put on the back burner. Just as the changes written into the Mammoth Law took years to generate, the next changes in education will be slow in coming. Some say no drastic innovations are likely to occur before the year 2000.

Erasmus of Rotterdam advocated moderation in all things and harmony among men.

CHAPTER 7

FOUR PORTRAITS

PICTURED HERE ARE portraits of four unique Dutch individuals. Stand before each of the portraits as you would in an art gallery and gaze at them. Although they appear to be unrelated, each is a brilliant splash of color and power in the mosaic of the gallery wall.

Desiderius Erasmus
(1469–1536)

Book bag dangling from the saddle, Desiderius Erasmus traveled on his horse from one foreign university to another to use the libraries and talk with his intellectual peers. Rarely did he return to his native land, where he found the people boorish, preoccupied with food and drink, and not much interested in matters of the spirit.

Born in Rotterdam to an unwed priest and his housekeeper, Erasmus was ordained a priest in the Augustine monastery of Steyn near Gouda, worked briefly as secretary to an archbishop, and studied the rest of his life.

He steeped himself in classical literature. The ancients, he felt, had long ago put forward the humanist view of the dignity of man, the only sentient being endowed with reason. Not only did this capacity entitle man to respect, but it also commanded him to respect his fellows.

Along with the humanities Erasmus studied the Bible and urged the Catholic Church to go back to the Holy Book. The church was riddled with superstitions and rigid with formalities. Priests failed to educate, while popes went to war.

Erasmus abhorred war. He quoted the Roman poet Ovid, who wrote, "Ambitions, avarice, and petulance impel even brothers to assail each other so that there is more harmony even among beasts. What serpent ever tried to poison another serpent? Does the lion prey on the lion, the wolf on the wolf?" Erasmus quoted the Apostle Paul, "Live in harmony with one another," and urged arbitration in conflicts, mutual understanding, and nonviolence.

He learned Greek so that he could supervise the printing of the New Testament in Greek. Only manuscripts too precious to move from country to country existed at the time. After paraphrasing Saint Paul's epistles, he had them translated into several vernaculars. "The sacred works should be in the hands of the farmer, the tailor, the traveler, and the Turk," he said. When the fear was voiced that the Bible might land in unsavory places, Erasmus expanded the list to include prostitutes and pimps. "Do you think that the Scriptures are only fit for the perfumed?"

Princes, popes, cardinals, and kings were honored by a visit from the urbane, witty leader of the liberal reform movement. Scholars thought their fame incomplete if they did not have at least one letter to prove that they were in correspondence with the great man. Dürer, Holbein, and Matsijs clamored to paint his likeness.

In spite of his renown, Erasmus was often short of money. Papal dispensations freed him from residing in Steyn and from the disability of being a bastard, thus clearing the way to posts and professorships. When these were offered to Erasmus, he declined. "They would keep me from my studies." Instead, he flattered the rich and influential into giving him a stipend or benefice, and he tutored the sons of the highly placed. To his tutoring we owe many of his published writings.

In *Adagia* he collected the ancients' proverbs and expressions, which soon became current in every European tongue, including English: "As many men, as many minds"; "where there is smoke, there is fire"; "many hands make light work." No doubt some of the sayings the Dutch are so fond of using were introduced into the Dutch language by Erasmus. From an initial eight hundred adages, the work grew to three thousand in later editions.

Erasmus wrote on the education of women, most of whom could not read or write. He went far beyond the notion of mere literacy and suggested that the mind of the adolescent girl be filled with study. After marriage, her interests should be cultivated. "Her husband will rejoice in a partnership on an intellectual level." In his writings he gave advice on politeness, conversation, and writing. He also wrote discourses on the prerequisites of a Christian ruler, confession, prayer, preaching, and the celibacy of priests. "Only a few are chaste. The unchaste would do better to acknowledge their children and give them a liberal education. I do not say that those who are ordained should get married. It were better that they devote themselves exclusively to the Church, but, if they cannot contain themselves, better that they marry."

His now best-known work, still read in college classes, is the satire *Encomium Moriae* in Greek, or *Praise of Folly*. Erasmus called it "just a little fantasy" tossed off in a week for the diversion of his English friend, Thomas More. He and Erasmus often joked in Latin, the second language of the educated—much to the chagrin of Mrs. More, who spoke only English. The title in Greek is a pun that can also be translated as "Praise of More."

Folly has lost little of her relevance today. With her retinue of Self-love, Pleasure, Flattery, and Sound Sleep,

Folly represents youth, vitality, happiness, and freedom from care. Happiness is the prerogative of the young, she says, and of all those subversive of dignity, hierarchy, and authority. Erasmus balances his lighthearted look at human foolishness with serious censure of the theological establishment.

The Catholic Church was in trouble; the Reformation was in full swing. As the rift between Catholics and Protestants deepened, an aging, frail Erasmus continued to preach harmony. Although critical of much that went on within the Catholic Church, he never broke with it. Although approving of much that Luther had to say, he never openly endorsed this reformer. During Erasmus's last, lonely years, the Catholics rejected him as subversive, and the Protestants as evasive. In the wave of religious persecutions friends like Thomas More lost their heads on the block. "My foes increase, my friends decrease," wrote Erasmus. He died in Basel, speaking his final two words in Dutch, *"Lieve God"* ("Dear God").

Vincent van Gogh
(1853–1890)

Where dark green cypresses line the radiant wheat fields of French Provence, its cobalt blue sky swept clear by a cutting dry mistral, you can easily imagine van Gogh with his straw hat and stubbly red beard sitting behind his easel in the blazing sun.

This tormented, unhappy man produced close to two thousand works of art in ten years, from the charcoal drawings and dark gloomy oils of his early Dutch period to the vibrant, explosive canvases of his years in France.

Of his somber *Potato Eaters* he wrote, "I have tried to emphasize that these people, eating their potatoes in the lamplight, have dug the earth with those very hands they put into the dish, and so it speaks of manual labor, and how they have honestly earned their food. I have wanted to give the impression of a way of life quite different from that of us civilized people. Therefore I am not at all anxious for everyone to like or to admire it at once."

About his landscapes he remarked, "Even if I paint them, I see figures in them. . . . After it snowed I saw cabbages in the fields. They reminded me of a group of women I had seen that morning in their thin skirts and old shawls at a water-and-fire cellar [a shop where hot water and burning peat embers were sold]."

When van Gogh took his life at the age of thirty-seven, only two of his works had been sold. Brother Theo inherited the collection. Most works were stored away in the attic, lined up on the floor. One shudders to think of what were to become priceless masterpieces gathering dust.

Theo died six months after Vincent, but his widow exhibited some of the paintings and later van Goghs fetched fantastic prices. Most of Vincent's works, however, were given to the Dutch state. Some hang in the Kröller-Müller Museum in the national park De Hoge Veluwe. In 1972 a Van Gogh Museum was opened in Amsterdam. Here his admirers come by the hundreds of thousands to sit quietly in front of a self-portrait or a luminous landscape.

The man who failed in his first calling as a preacher among the Belgian mine workers, whose desperate personal relationships ran aground throughout most of his life, now reaches the entire world through his art, as profoundly perhaps as Rembrandt, who was van Gogh's earliest and deepest source of inspiration.

Dr. Aletta H. Jacobs
(1854–1929)

Aletta Jacobs rocked the world of Dutch burghers by announcing her serious intention to go to the university to become a doctor. In the 1870s women did not become doctors, and universities were only for men. Aletta went all the way to the Dutch prime minister to obtain permission to attend the university.

The faculty reserved a room for her to sit in between classes, decorously away from the men. Aletta refused it. Hadn't she been raised in a family of brothers? She also refused to take the private anatomy lessons offered her because, she was told, it would not be proper for a woman to sit with men and learn about male anatomy. When Aletta Jacobs passed her final exams as the first woman doctor in The Netherlands, she made newspaper headlines.

From her home in Amsterdam where she set up practice, she walked in the evening to patients' homes, much to the concern of patrolling policemen. In those days prostitutes were the only women who walked unescorted on the street after dark. She went alone to the theater in defiance of the rule, "Women without male escorts are not admitted." Women who had no husband or brother to comply with this rule usually went to the theater with a station porter paid by the hour. In her memoirs Aletta Jacobs commented on the absurdity of an escort paid by the hour, and added "besides, I felt completely able to protect myself."

Photos show Dr. Jacobs as a petite woman, not averse to jewelry, ruffled collars, and picture hats. Behind this frilly facade was a woman with strong opinions on a range of subjects, including the prevailing Dutch marriage vows. She did not believe in them. "They make the woman promise obedience to the man and make her financially dependent on him." She would gladly have gone into a "living arrangement" with Carel Gerritsen if she and Carel had not wanted to spare the eventual child they both desired the "consequences of our action in defiance of the current ideas of morality." The two went to the registrar and were married.

The baby they wanted so badly lived but a day. Both had their work, used their own names, paid for their own clothes and books, and at the end of the year shared the household expenses. In the evening the couple read to each other the speeches they planned to give or the articles they planned to publish. Carel was as much a social reformer as Aletta.

With an unshakable belief that while all beginnings are difficult and that perseverance is required, reason and common sense will win out in the end, she argued for birth control, better housing and hygiene for the working classes, and equal pay for men and women. How surprised she had been when patients questioned her first doctor's bills on the assumption that she should charge less than male doctors. She joined women in other countries to obtain the women's vote and to work for peace.

At international congresses, where she met her American fellow-feminists Susan B. Anthony and Jane Addams, Carel Gerritsen was usually introduced as "Dr. Jacobs's husband" This caused him to remark "I understand now how a wife must feel when she can never be herself, when she is always treated as an appendage of her husband."

Dr. Jacobs also worked for the banning of legalized prostitution, which she considered demeaning for women and dangerous for national health. She was unsuccessful. To this day it is permitted in certain sections of Dutch cities, provided the prostitutes undergo a medical examination regularly. She did get chairs for shopgirls. In the face of vitriolic criticism, she dispensed simple contraceptives to women. She helped improve housing and working conditions for the working classes. Ten years before her death she was gratified that after decades of campaigning, Dutch women got the vote.

Their emancipation was slow. Not until 1958 could a married woman sign a check without the co-signature of her husband. Only in 1970 was the age of marriage without parental consent lowered from thirty to twenty-one for women. The matter of equal pay is still unresolved. But when at the fiftieth anniversary of Aletta Jacob's death a balance was taken, it was encouraging. Overall, the status of Dutch women, partially through her dauntlessness, has improved immeasurably.

Piet Mondrian
(1872–1944)

"Always further" was Mondrian's motto, and he devoted his whole life to perfecting his concept of art. He began with dark, thickly painted canvases of trees, windmills, and lighthouses in a style reminiscent of van Gogh. Then Mondrian went to Paris, and, influenced by Picasso and Léger in their cubist period, started to abstract the diversity of natural forms. Gradually, curved lines and obtuse or acute angles disappeared from his compositions, leaving grids of horizontal and vertical lines.

Back in The Netherlands, he and others founded a group that called itself *De Stijl* ("The Style") in 1917. The group's magazine of the same name published their manifesto: to eliminate all subjective observation of nature, to do away with art based on an "inner necessity," and to reduce art to the three primary colors (red, yellow, and blue) and the three nonprimary colors (white, gray, and black).

After breaking with the Stijl group, Mondrian carried their concept so far that he wanted each canvas to be a little world in itself, a world of harmony, of color and lines, stripped of anything fortuitous in nature so that only a general memory of its grandeur remained. In his search for a "true vision of reality," he even temporarily abandoned color. One of his most famous works is a composition of only five black connecting lines of varying thickness on a background of white.

Some art critics have assumed that Mondrians's rectilinear works were inspired by the forms and shapes of his native land, such as the tulip fields in spring. In *Piet Mondrian*, Dr. Hans L. C. Jaffé, professor of twentieth-century art at the University of Amsterdam, denies this. Dr. Jaffé concedes that Mondrian's art is affected by the Dutch landscape, but not on a visual plane. The Dutch landscape is not natural, but man-made. Generations have altered the land and actually created it. Mondrian's work also defies nature. He has created something in his own domain with the same precision, neatness, and feeling for measure and distance that the Dutch needed to create their straight canals, roads, and dikes.

For his fiftieth birthday, Mondrian's friends arranged a retrospective exhibition of his works in Amsterdam. His next show was in New York in 1942 when, at the age of seventy, he was still working to perfect his style. His last painting, although looking beautifully complete to the lay observer, was far from finished according to Mondrian. He painted *Victory Boogie-Woogie* in anticipation of the end of World War II. In it, the strictly linear pattern has become less important. The squares flow. The primary colors are back, bright and happy. The painting seems to vibrate with the rhythm of the big city, the tall buildings, the straight streets, and exuberant joy for the victory over tyranny.

During his lifetime Mondrian had little following, but now versions of his abstract designs can be seen on wallpaper, drapery fabric, scatter rugs, decorative pillows, and wall graphics. We have become so accustomed to seeing these patterns that we forget that they are to a large extent the products of the lifework of Piet Mondrian.

The sign announces "fine smoked Lake IJssel eel, warm smoked herring, etc."

CHAPTER 8

ALL BEGINNINGS ARE DIFFICULT

"*ALLE BEGIN IS MOEILIJK*," a Dutch friend may chuckle as you start learning Dutch and try pronouncing it.

Take the gutteral *g* as in Scheveningen, the beach resort near The Hague. You have to pull it, rumbling and hissing, from deep in your throat.

Not one Dutch vowel sounds the same as in English. It helps if you know some French or German. The *a* in the Dutch *amen* is bright and clear, like the *a* in the French *amour* ("love") or the German *aber* ("but"). The *u* in *uren* ("hours") sounds like the *u* in the French *tu* ("you") or the German *über* ("over"). The diphthongs, however, don't have their equal in any language with which you are likely to be familiar. The things not only look odd (*eu, ou, au, ij, ei*), but some of them also come in trios (*ieu, oei*). It takes practice to say them with ease, and you may raise an eyebrow if you don't pronounce them correctly. Suppose, for instance, that you want to tell a woman that her daughter is *leuk* (a much-used informal word that means nice), and as you struggle to make the *e* and the *u* into one sound, the word comes out as la-uk. The woman looks perplexed; she understood *lelijk* (la-luk), which means "ugly."

Pronunciation isn't the only difficulty in learning to speak Dutch. Each noun takes a definite article which may be *de* or *het*, and you have to remember which one is appropriate for each noun. The table is *de tafel*, the chair is *de stoel*, but the horse is *het paard*. Count your blessings, though. In plurals the definite article is always *de*, so you can't go wrong: *de tafels*, *de stoelen*, *de paarden*. And when you add *-je* to a noun (or *-tje*, or *-dje*, or *-pje*, depending on the noun's last letter) to make it a diminutive, the noun always takes *het*. The little table is *het tafeltje*, the little chair is *het stoeltje*, and the little horse is *het paardje*.

The Dutch make generous use of diminutives, and they are not at all particular about whom or what they make small. *Het meisje* ("the girl") may be six feet tall. *Mijn liefje* ("my little darling") could be a big, buxom matron. When parliament is opened by the queen, TV broadcasters report that the "little Orange sun" is shining or not shining, as the case may be. A diminutive is sometimes disparaging. *Wat een dagje* means "what a [bad] day!" A *fietsenmakertje*, in spite of the word's imposing length, is an "insignificant bike repair man."

A challenge when you speak Dutch is the correct use of the two forms of *you:* the informal *je* or *jij* (singular) or *jullie* (plural) and the formal *u* for both singular and plural. Not even the Dutch can give you a standard answer on when to use which. An adult addresses a child with *je*. A child addresses an adult with *u*, but if the adult is his parent the child may say *je*. This depends on the family's background and educational philosophies.

For many Dutch it is unthinkable that adults upon meeting each other would not use *u* and not call each other *Meneer*, *Mevrouw*, or *Juffrouw* ("Mr.," "Mrs.," or "Miss"). At the next meeting it remains "Mr." and "Mrs." and on through the years unless some day the elder says to the younger, or the woman to the man, "Shall we drop the *u*?" In an old-fashioned courtship this is a significant and delightful milestone the English language does not offer. She says coyly, "Won't you drop the *u*?" and he knows he is making progress.

On the other hand, don't be surprised if everyone you are introduced to at a party says *je* and calls you immediately by your first name.

Do be alert about the way the Dutch tell time when you are invited to a party. Dinner at "half past six" in English is said as "half seven" in Dutch, and many a foreign guest has come an hour late. To be on the safe side, try to get the invitation in writing. If your host or hostess uses the twenty-four hour clock, familiar to any American who has been in the navy, half past six appears as 18:30. If the date is added, remember that February 3 is written as 3/2 not as 2/3 as in English. So dinner at 6:30 on February 3 thus reads 18:30, 3/2.

In reading Dutch, beware of the different use of commas and periods in decimal figures. The Dutch write two thousand Dutch guilders as Hfl., Fl., F., or f. 2.000,00 rather than 2,000.00. In a business deal you might have a surprise if you read the Dutch figures wrong.

In reading Dutch you'll notice a fondness for long words. Don't panic when you see *stadsvernieuwingsgebied* or *garnalenspoelsorteermachine* or *paddestoelenbewegwijzeringsprogramma.* Just dissect the linguistic monsters into their component parts. The *stadsvernieuwingsgebied* is a *gebied* ("area") for *vernieuwing* ("renovation") of a *stad* ("town"). The *garnalenspoelsorteermachine* is a *machine* to *spoel* ("rinse") and *sorteer* ("sort") *garnalen* ("shrimps"). And that thirty-six letter word is a *programma* for the *bewegwijzering* ("marking roads with signs") having *paddestoelen* ("mushrooms"), the low mushroom-shaped trail markers of the Royal Dutch Touring Club.

Long Dutch words are often enmeshed in sentences that go on and on from comma to comma until a period finally comes in sight. Even the Dutch get impatient with them. "Please express yourselves in understandable language," wrote the law students of the Erasmus University in Rotterdam to the venerable Council of State. "Don't pile one subordinate clause on top of another." But so far, voices for brevity have been crying in the wilderness.

Dutch spelling is distinctive, too. You may receive letters from three generations in one Dutch family, and all three writers may spell differently. Grandpa, who went to school before the "new simplified spelling" mandated by a 1934 law, stays with the spelling he grew up with and writes *loopen* (two *o*'s) for "walk" and *flesch* (with a silent *ch*) for "bottle." His son, who may be one of the tens of thousands of Dutch youngsters who had to learn how to spell all over again in the middle of their school years, uses the official new spelling— *lopen* (with one *o*) and *fles* (without the *ch*). His son, born after World War II, not only uses the 1934 spelling, but he has also adopted several unofficial postwar phonetic spelling changes in words of foreign derivation. He writes *sjokolade* ("chocolate") instead of *chocolade* and *ekskuus* ("excuse") instead of *excuus*. Dad and Grandpa, however, think that the new phonetic spelling is abominable and still write these words in the traditional way.

Which spelling is the student of Dutch going to endorse? Obviously not the old spelling—it's obsolete and impractical. He will have to settle for the new official spelling and make his own choices about the spelling of foreign words. The options are given in "the little green book" that lies on the desk of every Dutch person who writes business letters. It's the *Woordenlijst Nederlandse Taal* ("Wordlist for the Dutch Language"), published for the Dutch and the three million Belgians who also speak Dutch by the Dutch State Printing Office. It gives the spelling options, plurals of nouns, diminutives if applicable, and which nouns take *de* or *het*.

By now it should be clear that in spelling as in politics, the Dutch deem that they are entitled to their own opinion. And they feel the same way about addressing letters. Unwieldy archaic forms are still observed by enough people that each pocket diary contains a section that lists eighty positions in society—from burgomaster and baron to pharmacist and physician—keyed by number to twenty-seven correspondence titles.

A lawyer with the academic degree of *Mr.* is *De Weledelgestrenge Heer* ("the very noble, upright gentleman") Mr. J. C. W. Huppeldepup. A man who has the Dutch equivalent of a Ph.D. degree and therefore precedes his name with *Dr.* is *De Weledelzeergeleerde Heer* ("the very noble, very learned gentleman") Dr. A. W. Jansen. A noble widow rates *De Hoogwelgeboren Vrouwe Douairière* ("the high, well-born lady dowager") Barones Zinderen van Zonderen-van Hovelingen tot Hogenraad. (Douairière is French for "dowager," a souvenir from the days when French words in the Dutch language were chic.) Behind the hyphen is the lady's maiden name which the Dutch tack onto any woman's married name in written address.

Unless you have a job in a Dutch office where this complicated form of address is obligatory, you may ignore the historic rigmarole and join the many people who address the lawyer simply as Mr. J.C.W. Huppeldepup, the man with the doctorate as Dr. A. W. Jansen, and the noble widow as Barones Zinderen van Zonderen-van Hovelingen tot Hogenraad.

People who do not have particularly elevated positions in life and who do not have academic degrees or noble predicates are addressed as *De Heer* ("Mr."), *Mevrouw* ("Mrs."), or *Mejuffrouw* ("Miss"). *Mw.* may be used for either a Mrs. or a Miss.

As you listen to the Dutch speak, you'll notice that even among the highly educated not everyone speaks standard Dutch. Speakers from below the rivers have that soft *g* that makes Dutch sound so much softer and more musical than the gutteral *g* of the north. Groningers clip the endings of their verbs. A Hagenaar gives himself away by what those who do not live in The Hague call his "la-di-da" speech.

Some accents stem from the regional dialects the Dutch still speak in scattered rural areas. "Why don't you speak your own language," an old farmer says to his son, who returns from the big city speaking standard Dutch.

Only in Friesland schools is the local dialect taught along with Dutch. *Frysk* is Friesland's second official language— or Friesland's first official language if you look at it from the viewpoint of the four hundred thousand Frysk-speaking Frisians. That's why you'll see all town signs in Friesland with two names and posters with the Frisian flag and the motto, *"praet mar frysk"* ("do speak Frisian"). Bilingual schools are a recent development, brought about by much campaigning in The Hague by the Frisian Movement, the Frisian Academy, and other organizations for the promotion of the Frisian cultural heritage. And so the Frisians have proved the Dutch proverb, "Who perseveres, wins."

The language is loaded with proverbs. Instead of Ben Franklin's maxim, "Early to bed, early to rise, makes a man healthy, wealthy, and wise," the Dutch say poetically, "Early morning has gold in its mouth." Many of their proverbs rhyme in Dutch for added charm, and not surprisingly, many proverbs are associated with wind and windmills, dikes and water:

Who comes first, mills first. (In medieval times a tenant farmer stood in line to have his grain ground in the windmill of his feudal lord who had the wind privilege, which permitted him to have a windmill and make the farmers pay for the use of the wind).

That's wheat for his windmill (that's to his advantage).

To receive the wind from the front (to be reprimanded).

As the wind blows, so blows his coat (his opinion or behavior is determined by circumstances).

He has been hit by a windmill (is a bit nutty).

That doesn't put sods on the dike (doesn't help).

Water has almost reached the top of the dike (a person is close to tears).

He got there with his heels over the canal (just made it).

He won't walk over one night's ice (is cautious).

When the calves are dancing on the ice (never).

He is as healthy as a fish.

To fish behind the net (to be too late for success).

He who wants to fish at night has to dry his nets during the day.

In times of storm one gets to know one's crew.

To come home with a wet sail (to swagger drunkenly; sailors used to wet their sails before tacking).

To go straight through the sea (to be honest).

The Dutch language reveals a great deal about the Dutch people. The regional accents in so small a country speak for their individualism, as do the variations in their spelling. Their formal terms of address speak of the Dutch penchant for detail, while the alternate informal usage indicates a desire to change the rigid structures of the past. And their proverbs, which laud the virtues of discipline, thrift, and caution, are clothed in the images of the wind and sea, at once the source of wealth and trouble.

In Rotterdam, cork, wood, and zinc from faraway lands await loading into a coaster and river barges for further transport. Landmark Euromast is in the background.

CHAPTER 9

FROM GALLEONS TO TUGBOATS

IN ROMAN TIMES ancestors of the Dutch sailed scows up and down the Rhine and its branching waterways to trade animal skins, goose feathers, and blonde braids for wine, coins, and glass. Important barter centers were Mosae Trajectum, Noviomagus, and Ultra Trajectum—settlements now known as Maastricht, Nijmegen, and Utrecht.

Trade continued through the Dark Ages, and by the seventeenth century the Dutch were sailing squat, square-rigged galleons to their trading posts in the New World and the Orient. Ships returned laden with beaver skins, exotic spices, silk, and holds crammed with wheat and ore. Merchants sold most of these goods abroad again.

For the Dutch, international trade has always been a matter of economic survival. To be able to afford importing the raw materials they lack, they must export; and for the sake of a sound economy, they must try to have as much money come into the country from the exports as goes out for the imports to maintain their balance of payments.

Currently the Dutch export about half of what they grow, raise, and above all, manufacture. Industry was stepped up drastically after World War II and now employs 40 percent of the work force.

Sold around the world are such things as kitchenwares, precision instruments, and baroque pipe organs. Magnificent instruments made by Flentrop in Zaandam fill the chapel of

Duke University in Durham, North Carolina, and Saint Mark's Cathedral in Seattle with glorious sounds.

Flentrop is a small, independent firm and an exception to the present trend. To better withstand growing world competition, many Dutch firms have pooled their resources and know-how in mergers, and they have not shied away from foreign capital. Swedish Volvo rescued Dutch Daf from bankruptcy. The firm makes trucks and automobiles with a unique system of variomatic gears. Fokker, which makes Friendship turboprops and Fellowship jets, merged with a German firm. Germany, in fact, is now strongly interconnected with various industrial activities in The Netherlands.

Foreign money has created giants like the Big Four: Royal Dutch, Unilever, AKZO, and Philips. These multinational corporations are praised by some for making a valuable contribution to social and economic fields and criticized by others for their awesome power in the world marketplace.

N.V. Koninklijke Nederlandsche Petroleum Maatschappij ("the Royal Dutch Petroleum Company"), one of the parents of the Royal Dutch/Shell group of companies, is the biggest of the four and is still 60 percent Dutch.

Number 2 is Unilever N.V., established in the 1870s by two North Brabant men who sold butter by the shipload to England. Unable to buy enough natural butter, they went into margarine. In 1927—after fierce rivalry—the Dutch margarine manufacturers joined forces in the Margarine Unie, and three years later they teamed up with Lever, a British soap-making firm. Unilever now has five hundred companies in seventy-five countries. It still produces soap and margarine as well as convenience foods like frozen pizzas, and canned hams, cosmetics, and animal feeds. Other interests include restaurants, chemicals, and transport.

AKZO N.V. has its "AKZO Seven," which are deep into chemical and pharmaceutical products. The group came about as the result of mergers in the late 1960s and already has 160 operations going in fifty countries.

N.V. Philips' Goeilampenfabrieken is the only one of the Big Four that still headquarters exclusively in The Netherlands. It was founded in Eindhoven, where Gerard Philips began making *gloeilampen* ("electric bulbs") in 1891 with a staff of ten. Now 380,000 employees on six continents produce Philips radios, TV equipment, records, medical equipment, computers, and all types of electronic equipment. Philips is the Dutch "Ford Story."

Other industries are faring less well these days. Take shipbuilding, for example.

Once the Dutch were the absolute masters. Foreign nations ordered sailing vessels by the fleet. Now other countries build good ships for less, and their labor costs are lower. The Dutch shipbuilding industry, which once sustained world trade, continues on a diminished scale in Flushing and Amsterdam.

Here the Dutch fill precious orders for containerships, platforms for oil rigs in the sea, and the freighters which, for the most part, are used by the Dutch themselves.

The Dutch shipping industry has also declined. Before World War II, The Netherlands was among the five top shipping nations of the world, but now only the oceangoing tugboats maintain their leading position. Tough little tugs tow anything that floats. They may haul a drydock from Amsterdam to Singapore, or an oil production island from the Gulf of Mexico to the North Sea.

Smit Internationale Nederland BV, the largest of the oceangoing tugboat firms, even towed a floating paper factory, complete with power plant, from Japan to a river in the interior of Brazil. The client was an American company that wished to cut and pulp its Brazilian timber growth on the site. Smit also tows icebergs away from Arctic oil rigs and now there are plans for towing icebergs to the Middle East to aid in water supply. Fanciful talk for "Holland's Glory"? That's what Jan de Hartog called the tugboat men in his novel of the same name. The book appeared in The Netherlands during World War II, and de Hartog made such national heroes of his brave tugboat men while their real-life counterparts were manning tugboats for the Allies that the Germans couldn't stand it and forbade the book's sales.

Fishing, like shipbuilding, is no longer the mainstay of the Dutch economy that it once was, when envious neighbors said, "The Hollanders find gold in the sea." Competition has increased, and radar guides fishermen of many nations to the shoals. As a result, the herring population has gone down at an alarming rate, and in 1977 the North East Atlantic Fishing Commission of the Common Market decreed a closed herring season on the North Sea. For the first time in Dutch fishing history, the sea was not free.

Fewer than fifty Dutch herring trawlers now cruise the Atlantic as far north as Iceland. Some four hundred fifty cutters go as far south as the Bay of Biscay for plaice and sole, whereas a hundred fifty little shrimp boats throw their nets off the Dutch coast and in the Wadden Sea. That is what's left of the once impressive Dutch fishing fleet.

The freshwater fishermen who catch eel, perch, and pike in Lake IJssel and the Zeeland estuaries have problems of their own. Fish are dying from lack of oxygen and dangerous chemicals, most probably originating in the Rhine.

The romantic river that has its source high in the Swiss Alps, wends its way past vineyard-covered hills through Germany, and slices through The Netherlands to empty into the North Sea, has become the biggest open sewer in Europe. All along its course industries dump refuse in the river, and only a few can afford sewage purification plants. The Rhine countries have been talking for years about more stringent regulations, but so far significant action has not been taken. Something will have to be done. Safe Rhine water is vital to all the nations along the Rhine. In The Netherlands not only fishermen need clean Rhine water: one-third of the Dutch population drink water that comes from the Rhine, and farmers spray their fields with it.

The Dutch refer to the river as "Our Rhine," but on maps it is called the Waal after it enters the country at the German border, and then it becomes the Waterweg for its final length, which is a canal linking Rotterdam with the North Sea. A branch of the river known as the Neder-Rijn ("Lower Rhine") becomes the Lek, a tributary that funnels into the Waterweg.

"Our Rhine" is a busy place. During 1977 the Ministry of Water counted 215,000 ships on the Waal at Nijmegen. This works out to a frequency of about two ships per minute during working days. Skippers rarely sail at night or on Sundays.

Tankers slide majestically by pugnacious little tugboats pushing a string of open barges. When barges sail under their own power, the skipper and his family live on board in a tiny space near the steerage, astern of the enormous hold. It is not unusual to see diapers drying on a line and a baby boxed in a firmly anchored playpen.

Many of the barges pick up or deposit freight in Rotterdam's harbor, significantly called Europort. It rose from the ruins of World War II and for the past several years has earned the title, "The World's Biggest Port."

As tooting tugboats bring enormous ships to their berths, bow waves and wakes churn up the harbor water. On the quais, tall elevator cranes swing loads from huge wheat terminals into the ships. A dapper little boat puts a floating screen around an oil spill to prevent it from spreading and commandeers a pump boat to suck up the oil. The culprit, when known, pays for the cleaning.

Along the shores of the Waterweg, crude oil is refined in a weird, silent world of pipes, scaffolds, and vats. Flares and foul odors rise from slim chimneys. Rows of huge round storage tanks wait to be emptied by tankers.

By the early 1970s Europort ran out of space. The Dutch simply added land to the coast of the North Sea for more warehouses and more docks. Only the conservationists are angry. The chimneys of the new Meuse Plain "dirty the horizon," they say, and it's true that you can see them for miles as you walk along the beach.

Amsterdammers view Rotterdam's explosive postwar growth with jealousy. Once Amsterdam was a forest of masts, but now that the Zuiderzee is closed off, ships can reach the harbor only through the North Sea canal after they pay fees at the IJmuiden locks. Nevertheless, Amsterdam is still the nation's second-ranking international port, followed by young Eemsport in the province of Groningen.

The Dutch need these international ports so they can earn more foreign money. For the same reason, tourists are welcomed in The Netherlands; worldwide offices of ABN, the General Bank of The Netherlands, loan capital; Dutch insurance firms write policies; and the Dutch airline KLM flies passengers for thousands of miles. Without the dollars, marks, and yen paid for these services, the Dutch would forever have an unfavorable balance of trade.

"Our invisible export" they call the services, and with it they lump the exportation of Dutch knowledge.

Technicians and business persons fly around the world to sell their expertise, much as Jan Leeghwater counseled European sovereigns on draining marshes in the seventeenth century. Jan's twentieth-century counterparts have made proposals for urban development in Karachi, Pakistan, and designed a gigantic Iraq irrigation scheme. In Java, the immense Buddhist shrine of Borobudur, which was built in the ninth century, is being restored for the Indonesian government. In Tanzania, hundreds of villages have been provided with shallow wells and easy-to-operate pumps to replace crude and unsanitary water holes. Engineers from the Ministry of Water and the Hydraulic Laboratory of the University of Delft joined the consulting team.

The Dutch help to plan such projects and send experts with equipment. Local labor does the work while the World Bank, the United Nations Development Fund, or the European Development Bank provides loans or grants.

Now Dutch consulting firms hope to sell their expertise to the People's Republic of China. A channel has to be dug in the mouth of the Yangtse River so that large ships can sail upstream to a steel factory, and an area of 250,000 acres at the mouth of the river will be diked in for farming land. In Lien Yun Kang, four hundred miles north of Shanghai, the Chinese want a seaport built near the largest coal reserves in China.

So the Dutch energetically work towards maintaining their balance of payments on which their economy stands or falls.

Labor relations are good. The country has had no long, crippling strikes. The bonanza of natural gas found in Dutch soil in the 1960s has enabled the Dutch to sell large quantities abroad with long-term contracts. Gas is piped all the way to Italy.

The economy, however, is not as robust as it was in the sixties after the Dutch had revived it almost miraculously from its moribund postwar state. The people of this crowded land will need the wisdom of Solomon to determine how to meet the economic needs of various special interest groups while benefiting the nation as a whole.

They will also need the world economy on their side.

A vast field of red and white Triumph tulips growing near Haarlem.

CHAPTER 10

CHEESE AND TULIPS

TWICE A DAY in every province of The Netherlands, farmers'
hands or milking machines squirt rich streams of milk from
heavy udders. For years, clusters of shiny metal milk cans
waited along country roads for pickup by dairy factory
trucks. Now farmers are switching to the use of refrigerated
vats from which factory drivers siphon the milk directly into a
refrigerated tank car. Soon the familiar sentinels of every
dairy farmer's driveway will be gone.

Except in winter, when the plump black and white cows
are in their barns, you'll see them almost as soon as you leave
a Dutch town. There are four million cows in The Netherlands, which works out to about 1 cow to every 3.5
inhabitants. Almost half of the tiny country is under grass for
the benefit of these cows, but cattle contribute less than 5
percent to the gross national product. Why is there such an
extravagant use of space instead of feed lots?

The Dutch need quality cheese and butter for export in
their never-ending struggle to maintain the balance of
payments, and only lush green pastures will do for cows that
are the top milk producers in the world. Chrome-filled
factories turn their milk into butter and Edam, Leiden,
Gouda, and farmer's cheese. Edams the size of bowling balls
weigh up to five pounds while cartwheels of Gouda may
weigh in at a hefty twenty.

Cheese lovers outside The Netherlands often find Dutch

cheese in their local delicatessens, but local stores do not carry the many flavor varieties that are available in the country itself. One can choose from many grades between "young" cheese, which has been left to mature on the factory shelf for just a few weeks, and *belegen* cheese, which has aged from six months to a year. Young cheese is soft, spongy, and bland, while belegen cheese is firm, dry, and pungent. Edam may be so old that it crumbles when it is sliced, and then its flavor is deliciously sharp.

Dutch shoppers tend to make a fuss about buying cheese, just as wine connoisseurs do when selecting their Bordeaux or Burgundy.

"Could I have a Gouda midway between young and belegen?" a shopper in a cheese shop may ask as the salesperson quickly pares a sliver off a big cartwheel.

"No, I'd like one a bit older," the shopper says after sampling the fare. Down goes the salesperson's hand again and pares a sliver from another cheese. The line of shoppers, with bulging nets and plastic bags dangling from their arms, wait patiently. They, too, are going to take their time with their pound of cheese.

Should one wish to buy an entire Edam or cartwheel, the salesperson plunges a cheese borer into the cheese and retrieves a sausagelike sample.

Today's cheese shops often carry "modern" cheese in addition to old-timers like Edam, which takes its name from a town on the Zuiderzee that was a prospering cheese port in the sixteenth century. Dutch bluefort is a new, milder version of the French Roquefort. During the ripening process the cheese is pierced with long skewers, and *penicillum roqueforti* is introduced into the channels to produce the characteristic blue mold. The Dutch cheese industry has also come up with Subenhara, a dessert cheese spiced with garlic and parsley and a name right out of *A Thousand and One Nights*.

If Dutch cheese gets around in the world, so do Dutch cattle. Dutch cows roam the steppes of Russia and the plains of Peru. In the United States, Holsteins are of Frisian descent.

Dutch bulls used to walk around those foreign pastures to help improve the local breed. Now their semen is collected at Dutch artificial insemination centers, placed in refrigerated vials, and airlifted abroad. The local cows are impregnated artificially.

Much of the Dutch breeding stock is raised in the northern province of Friesland, where the cattle industry has done so well that the bronze statue of a cow has been placed on a Leeuwarden square. *Ûs Mem* ("Our Mother"), as she is called, is supposed to have the ideal measurements. If two farmers at the weekly cattle market cannot agree on the proper size of a rump or a chest, they go to *Ûs Mem* and measure her—or so the story goes.

Cultivated land takes up another 20 percent of the precious national land. Potatoes, sugar beets, and cereal grains are the major crops, and they grow best on the heavy clay of the Low Netherlands polders. Crops are also doing well in the High Netherlands now that sandy soil is improved with chemical fertilizers.

How much and what the Dutch farmer plants each year, and who buys what he grows, largely depends on decisions made in Brussels. Here, at Common Market headquarters, experts from the nine member countries determine what is best for each nation. In this respect, The Netherlands has totally lost its sovereignty.

Because Brussels sets one price for agricultural products, the Dutch farmer has no worries about being undercut by another Common Market farmer. The Common Market subsidizes his product, and his cooperative guarantees the Dutch farmer the minimum Brussels-set price.

At a vegetable auction in the Westland near Rotterdam, a

barge heaped high with plump red tomatoes sails past buyers on a canal that goes right through the auction building. Since it is the last of many barges that have been auctioned off today, no one bids. The auctioneer "turns through" the tomatoes, and the farmer's cooperative pays him the minimum price. The unsold produce goes without charge to another farmer for cattle feed. Every branch of the agricultural industry has a private cooperative in which members help one another in this way.

With all this protection the Dutch farmer may appear to be in an enviable position, but he has to cope with one situation that's uniquely Dutch and not always attractive! Because of land reapportionment regulations, he may have to give up land that has been in his family for generations.

A land consolidation act, passed in 1954, restructures rural land where lots are too small to be worked with modern machinery and roads are too winding and narrow to carry it. Two farmers, both with several tiny parcels separated by each other's land, may both end up with one continuous property by selling the interfering parcels to each other through a mediating government agency. Or one farmer may sell all his land outright to another farmer so that the buyer can acquire property of efficient size. In such cases the dispossessed farmer may opt to be retrained for other work if he is young, while an older farmer may prefer to sell his tenant or property rights on paper and stay on the farm until he dies.

As farms increase in size, superfluous farmhouses are torn down and others modernized in what the Dutch call a *sanering* program. *Sanering* literally means "making healthy." Bulldozers come and push earth into a canal here and dig another canal somewhere else. Winding roads are straightened and widened. Clumps of age-old trees, however, are carefully preserved, and new farmhouses are built in the traditional style of the region so that reapportionment does not mar the beauty of the countryside.

Because they already work at top efficiency on their tiny lots, vegetable farmers are usually not affected by land consolidation. A large family that has older children pitching in can live well on no more than three to five acres. The secret is high yield gardening in which four crops a year are grown under glass.

The Dutch take more time with their most famous horticultural product. Each fall gardeners in thirty-six countries plant a total of four billion Dutch bulbs. Their efforts are rewarded a few months later when crocuses and anemones announce the coming of spring. The riot of Dutch colors continues through summer with the blooming of gladioli, dahlias, and lilies. "Our best ambassadors abroad," the Dutch call them.

In The Netherlands, thousands upon thousands of foreign visitors come to the fields each spring to see the brilliant carpets where new bulbs flower. But it may happen that they see only leaves and cut stalks. As soon as "sick seekers" determine that plants are healthy, heads are chopped off so that the bulbs can retain their strength for other flowerings. The only color the visitor then sees is a bright red or yellow mountain sliding by on a canal boat. The lopped-off blooms are on their way to the garbage heap, except for those that local children string into garlands and sell as car hood decorations. There are always plenty of bulb fields left, however, where the blooms are "still on," and on "bulb weekends" from early March to late May, the traffic is bumper to bumper.

People who find a place to park walk through the "bulb villages" and admire the little Edens the local citizens have made of their front gardens with flowering bulbs. On the grass lie mosaics painstakingly put together from stripped hyacinth blooms. The year after John Kennedy was assassinated, such a striking likeness of the late president filled one lawn that Americans who came upon the portrait without warning wiped away tears.

For the epitome of flowering bulb delight, visitors go to Keukenhof, once the kitchen garden of a feudal countess. Now it is a wondrous sixty-acre park near Lisse. Here thousands of prize bulbs flower only for show. Harmonious clusters of them are spread over immaculate lawns among lovely old trees and statues overlooking still pools. The visitors walk along the paths in reverent silence as if they were sightseeing in an ancient church. Signs are posted showing a transistor radio slashed by a red line: no radios are allowed.

For very important persons like heads of state, hostesses wear costumes with white pointed coifs, tight bodices, and wide, ankle-length skirts. They look like Countess Jacoba probably did in her workclothes.

On a tour of Keukenhof the guide is likely to tell the tale of the tulip.

In the seventeenth century the Turks were cultivating the flower *tulipa*, which looked like a turban and grew wild in the hills. When the flowers were introduced to Western Europe, they soon became a status symbol. Ladies at the court of Louis XIV of France tucked tulips into their *décolletés*—the more expensive the tulip, the greater the woman's prestige. In the Republic of the United Netherlands, wealthy burghers tried to outdo each other in the sumptuousness of their tulip gardens. One cautious merchant rigged an alarm between his bed and the garden so that thieves wouldn't dig up his investments in the night.

Tulip bulbs soared in price. One called *Semper Augustus* ("Always the Exalted One") fetched four thousand Dutch florins. Three bulbs went for a house. Two bulbs netted two sacks of wheat, four sacks of rye, four oxen, eight pigs, twelve sheep, two barrels of wine, four barrels of beer, a hundred pounds of cheese, a bed with bedding, a suit, and a silver cup—which is far more than the Dutch had paid a few years earlier for a tract of land in the New World called Manhattan.

The tulipomania lasted three years and became the butt of cartoonists. One drew a tavern in the shape of a giant jester's cap with drooping peak and bells. Outside the tavern a man wearing another jester's cap pushes a wheelbarrow filled with weeds. "Picture of the strange year 1637 when one fool bred another fool, when people were rich without possessions, and wise without using their brains" is the legend for this caricature. The Dutch were buying bulbs on credit and selling bulbs they did not own. When the bottom suddenly fell out of the market, the speculators were ruined.

Sanity returned to the tulip industry, but the flower itself remained a luxury. Not until this century were tulip bulbs grown in such quantity that many could afford them.

During the tulipomania streaked tulips were the rage. Judith Leyster drew the most popular ones in color in a famous book on view in the Frans Hals Museum in Haarlem. Unfortunately, "feathering" turned out to be a virus symptom that soon killed the plants. Now tulips are mainly plain with different color "trim" on the anthers, the edges, and the insides of the petals. Varieties differ according to blooming time, stem length, and the number and shape of petals. There are so many combinations that twenty-seven hundred tulips have earned a place in the *Classified List and International Register of Tulip Names*.

The list begins with "*Aafje Heynis* (F. Rijnveld & Sons, Ltd.), exterior neyron-rose, edged primrose-yellow, inside primrose-yellow with neyron-rose to the base, base sulphur yellow edged blue, anthers purple, 1960." Even catalog readers who have never heard of neyron-rose will sense that *Aafje Heynis* is a spectacular tulip. One hundred and thirty pages later the book ends with "*Zwanenburg* (Van Tubergen, Ltd.), pure white, base white, anthers black, Haarlem, 1912."

In real life Aafje Heynis is a Dutch oratorio singer; Zwanenburg is the name of a garden. Tulips are named after queens, presidents, movie stars, and astronauts. One even takes its name from a magazine. When *Sunset*, an American periodical, celebrated its seventy-fifth birthday, an orange tulip was christened *Sunset*. In ceremonies at the Keukenhof, the magazine publisher's mother sprinkled it with champagne from a silver bowl.

Growers and merchants sell bulbs sight unseen or at bulb auctions "under the clock." The "clock" is a wooden board with a huge circle with figures from one to one hundred in the rim. As baskets of bulbs are held up to prospective buyers, an electric dial indicates the guilder and cents amounts called off by the auctioneer. He always begins with a high amount and goes down. When a number lights up on the clock, the dial stops. The buyer with that number has bought the lot for the price at which he stopped the dial by pressing a button in front of him.

Bunches of cut tulips are also sold under the clock at flower auctions like the big one in Aalsmeer.

Here all year long, six days a week, perfect blooms are trundled about on carts in vast halls and wheeled into one of several auction rooms. Visitors are allowed to stand behind glass above the bleachers where the wholesalers, retailers, and exporters sit with their hands near the decisive buttons. It's fun to hear the auctioneer call off amounts in a singsong voice, and see the bunches of tulips, roses, carnations, and chrysanthemums held up as samples of the floral richness on the carts.

The flowers sold at Aalsmeer are boxed and rushed to the

airport where they are shipped to Hamburg, Zürich, and Paris.

Inflation notwithstanding, flowers are still reasonably priced in The Netherlands. Every outdoor market has at least one flower stall. Flower vendors stand with carts at street corners, in stations, and in front of hospitals. Florist shops abound. Some are just little holes in the wall where each morning, except during extreme cold, the shop owner puts bunches of flowers in water-filled cans and buckets out on the sidewalk. Passersby have to squeeze by each other as they detour around the tempting displays.

The Dutch regularly buy flowers for their friends and for their homes, which they consider "empty" without a *bloemetje*. Flowers wrapped in paper are hand carried along the street, or lie across the handlebars of a bicycle. Flowers lie on the lap of a portly old lady in the streetcar, or are held high by a rugged fellow who stands squashed in the crowded aisle. Thanks to its flower-loving citizens, The Netherlands is in bloom even on the bleakest winter days.

The Squall by Willem van de Velde, Jr. Ships have been in the fabric of Dutch life for centuries and have inspired legends like "The Flying Dutchman."

CHAPTER 11

THE FLYING DUTCHMAN AND OTHER TALES

A SQUALL LIFTED the fully rigged ship out of the swirling trough and slammed it against a towering wave. Taut sails strained. Masts creaked. Water gushed over the deck. The ship listed, righted, and sailed on.

Alone on the bridge stood Captain van Straaten, the only man still alive on the ship.

The captain had thought he could defy the sea. Against all advice he set sail in a raging storm, but when his ship was near foundering, van Straaten had called upon the devil.

"I'll help you, captain," the devil said, "but you'll have to sail for me always in storms, within sight of land, never to set foot ashore."

Captain van Straaten had been sailing for centuries over the seas of the world. Weary of hearing the wind mock him as the devil once had done and pushed beyond the limits of his endurance by the sea, he wanted to die.

Now he was racing close to Scotland's craggy coast. An old fisherman peering into the darkness from the top of a cliff saw the contours of a ship with all sails spread. He ran down the steep, rocky path to the beach, untied his sloop and, pulling against the huge waves, came close to the ship. At the moment the captain threw him a line, the wind stopped. The clouds disappeared, and stars shone against the black sky. When the old man climbed the ship's ladder, the sea was mirror smooth.

Van Straaten guided the weary visitor to his cabin and poured him a mug of beer. They shared sea stories. Finally, the old man suggested that the captain come to his home on the cliff for a rest.

"I shall, dear man, but at dawn the wind will blow again, and I must be back on my ship."

They made their way to the small hut, and there before the fireplace sat the fisherman's daughter, stirring soup in a pot hanging over glowing embers. Her rippling hair was the color of golden wheat, and her skin had the pink and white freshness of spring blossoms. Her eyes were sky blue—the kind of blue the captain could hardly remember. Spellbound, the captain knelt before her and took her hand. She asked him who he was.

"I am van Straaten, a poor wretch doomed to sail the seas until the day of the last judgment. But the devil made a pact with me. One night every seven years I may go ashore to search for a woman's love that will lift my curse."

"All my life I have loved the man in the portrait you see there on the wall. It is as if you were he. Others have tried to win me, but I have known *he* would come for me from the sea. I shall sail with you, captain."

Now that he heard the blessed words that would end his curse, the price was too great. "No," he said. "I will not have you come. When the curse is lifted, I must die. You must, too, if you come with me."

They argued. She said she wanted to follow him. He said she couldn't go. Then he took her in his arms, looked once more into her sky blue eyes, and fled down the cliffs towards the sea. As if on signal, clouds, winds, and giant-crested waves carried him to the ship.

At the edge of the cliff stood Bridget, caught in the wind. She could barely see the captain as he climbed over the rail.

"I love you," she cried, and whispering to the devil, "I will die for him," she hurled herself into the sea.

The captain's ship broke in two. With a great, rending sigh, the *Flying Dutchman* gave up her life.

How many times Dutch elders must have told this tale to the children as they all sat near the peat fire and the wind whistled around the little houses behind the dike. The youngsters could well imagine what the sea of the *Flying Dutchman* looked like. Hadn't they stood on the dike and seen the waterwolf? Hadn't they heard tales about fathers and brothers of townsfolk who had sailed off?

No wonder so many legends were told in The Netherlands about sea captains and about the sea that brought them good and evil.

One captain from Stavoren, a thriving Frisian town on the Zuiderzee, was ordered by a wealthy merchant's widow to bring her the noblest, richest cargo he could find. Six months later he returned. When he showed her a hold full of golden wheat, "the staff of life," she spit in his face. "Why didn't you bring me silk, ebony, and jade?" Then she asked a puzzling question, "Over which side of the ship did you take that wheat on board, miserable captain?"

"Why, over the port side, my lady."

"Take your ship out of the harbor and throw all that trash over the starboard side."

"But, but—God won't approve of such waste. He will ruin you."

She drew a costly ring off her finger and tossed it into the harbor. "With all the ships I own, there is as little chance of my being ruined as there is for me to see this ring again."

The captain sailed his ship out of the port and slowly poured the precious wheat into the sea.

A few days later the Lady of Stavoren gave a great banquet. Servants carried in a huge fish, prepared with the rarest of herbs, on a shining silver platter. The guests stopped talking and watched as their hostess cut off the head. When she removed the skin and meat, there lay her glittering ring. Before the meal was over, a courier ran into the dining hall and told the lady that one of her ships had been ground to splinters in a storm in the Baltic. A second courier brought the news that pirates had captured a ship near Spain. Before the Lady of Stavoren went to bed that night, she learned that she had lost all her ships.

As for the captain's wheat, tall grassy weeds grow on a sandbar off Stavoren. People say they first sprouted from the wheat the luckless captain had to throw into the sea. The sandbar is known as Vrouwenzand ("Woman's Sand").

A few miles north of Stavoren lies the town of Hindeloopen, where the Wybes family bred a line of doughty sea captains. The mayor of Amsterdam once sent Captain Auke Wybes to Russia with a letter for the czar.

The captain approached the port of Saint Petersburg warily and hoisted a small pennant in one of the stays of his ship as a signal for a pilot. What did the Russians know, after all, about building ports or guiding experienced captains like Auke Wybes inside? He saw a small boat being rowed from the shore. The pilot, an unlikely looking sort with a big fur cap, climbed aboard the ship.

"What's your name, skipper, and from whence do you come?"

"I am Auke Wybes of Hindeloopen in Friesland."

"You are the first Dutch vessel to enter my brand-new port. I am granting you the privilege of entering it without paying harbor dues as long as the same keel will carry your ship. You will call it *Saint Petersburg* from now on."

Wybes understood then that his pilot was Czar Peter himself and gave him the letter.

The tall Russian broke the seals with the three *X*s of Amsterdam's coat of arms and quickly read the message.

"You bring good news, I shall not forget it."

Peter the Great kept his word. Whenever Auke Wybes came in port, he enjoyed the czar's protection and made advantageous deals. The toll-free privilege allowed him to buy furs and other goods at competitive prices. Auke Wybes returned from each Baltic voyage a richer man, fulfilling the first part of a Russian gypsy's prophecy that wealth would be his.

Wybes had only one son, whose godfather was the czar of Russia. When Peter Wybes's ship had to be replaced, he built a new one on the old keel; and when Peter's only son had to replace it, he built *his* new ship on the old keel.

The captains Wybes prospered. Plates of porcelain as thin as eggshell, pearls piled like marbles on pewter plates, and vases made of silver and gold filled the salon of their traditional Hindeloopen "captain's house."

Prosperity, however, did not bring lasting happiness to the third captain Wybes, who was named after the founder of the family fortune. When death took his young wife and infant son, Auke Wybes became a sad, embittered man.

When he returned home from his voyages, he did not even bother to hang the little anchor from the hook under the eave, as was the custom to announce to the townspeople that the captain was there. He locked himself in the house and kept the shutters closed so that he would not see the greed he imagined in the eyes of his neighbors. He believed they looked forward to the time when he would die without an heir and his riches would be divided among them. Each time he left his house after nightfall, he carried a box full of treasures and piled it onto a growing stack in his ship's hold.

Back and forth he sailed around Denmark and through the Baltic, until one dreary fall day when the *Saint Petersburg* returned again to the Hindeloopen port. The crew had been paid their wages and had gone off to spend their money. Carrying a burning lantern, the captain roamed through the hollow-sounding rooms of his house. When night came, he stuffed his remaining gold ducats in his coat pockets and boarded the ship. In his cabin he turned his pockets inside out and scattered the coins over the sloping floor. They came to rest in the dust against the bottom of his bunk. Then he found a torch, lit it with a sulfur match, and threw it into the hold.

Without a backward look, Captain Auke Wybes left his ship, untied her moorings, and quickly walked to his house.

The *Saint Petersburg* drifted off with the ebbing tide and burst into flames. Thus sank the ship on the keel that had carried three generations of captains Wybes.

"Auke Wybes, Auke Wybes, wake up, wake up! Your ship is gone!" The neighbors pounded against the shuttered windows. But Auke Wybes lay dead on his bed. From then on, the trade of Hindeloopen declined, and the second part of the Russian gypsy's prophecy to his grandfather came true: "Hindeloopen will fall asleep when the *Saint Petersburg* sinks into the sea."

In some of the Dutch legends about the sea and water, animals play a central role.

The time was when the waterwolf, with his bared white fangs, shaggy hair, and long shadow, loomed behind every dike and riverbank. But he is still too real to make a good story. Many Dutch living today have witnessed for themselves the wolf's insatiable hunger as he swallows farmland and villages.

A kindlier creature was the cat who kept a baby girl alive during the Saint Elizabeth's flood of 1421 by jumping from one side of her wooden cradle to the other as it floated among the debris. Everyone knows how cats hate water! Where the cat and the cradle allegedly touched ground, the town of Kinderdijk ("Child's Dike") now stands in a polder southeast of Rotterdam.

The tale of Lijsje and the colt of Volendam is a strange sort of love story that also has a happy, though eerie, ending.

As summer heat hung heavy in the air, a young horse suddenly appeared among the farmers' daughters who were pitching hay. Because he was dripping wet and holding a fish in his mouth, they thought he must have come from the Zuiderzee behind the dike.

All the girls were afraid of the strange colt except Lijsje, a lively lass with a bubbling laugh. She spoke to the colt with the same kind of sweet talk she used for the babies at home, and took the fish from him with the thought of how pleased her mother would be with just this much more to serve for the evening meal.

A clap of thunder followed a streak of lightning. The colt bolted over the dike, and when the girls reached the top to run home, the animal was nowhere in sight. Not even a ripple in the water hinted at where the colt must surely have gone.

Soon he became a regular visitor. He never forgot to bring Lijsje a fish, and she pulled the freshest grass she could find for him. He liked to stand near her and, nudging her neck with his head, waited to be scratched behind his ears or to have a kiss pressed on his soft nose.

"Ha, ha, look at Lijsje and her lover," passing boys taunted.

Then he stayed away from the fields for a long time. When he returned, he had grown into a magnificent animal with a long, silky tail. He seemed to want Lijsje to climb on his back. When she mounted the great horse, she sat high above the polder and looked down on the mounds onto which she had tossed hay with her fork. He took her to the top of the dike where he broke into a canter, and then he swerved, running like the wind to the sea. As her friends watched in horror, the sea folded over the horse and Lijsje. Her head appeared above the surface only once, and she waved joyously.

The young men of Volendam built ships to look for Lijsje. They threw out nets to find her corpse, and each night they returned with their nets full of fish. And so it came to pass that a poor farming village became a flourishing fishing village.

People in villages by the sea often supplemented their income by beachcombing. In a collection entitled *De Lachende Hollander,* Olaf J. de Landell retells one old tale about villagers who did more than walk the beach in the hope of a lucky find.

The story goes that on one of the Wadden Islands in the most northern part of The Netherlands, men would give false signals to ships at sea and cause them to run aground. If the cargo washed onto the beach, the islanders salvaged it. Since the ship's crew had drowned, what else could they do?

Then, perhaps because the new minister had made it so eloquently clear that the practice was sinful, no galleons were wrecked on the coast for a long time and no boxes with treasures washed ashore.

The islanders felt that something had to be done. Six of the most esteemed church members dressed up in their best breeches, coats with silk lapels, and silver-buckled shoes, and went to see the minister. The callers remarked on the weather, inquired after the minister's health, praised the quality of the grazing on the new polder, and seemed quite unable to state the reason for their visit. A silence fell. The dominie smiled. The men looked at each other. Which one of the six was going to say why they had come? At last one of them stuttered, "Dominie, don't be angry with us, but it has been so long since we had a shipwreck, couldn't you pray for one next Sunday?"

The dominie was bewildered. How could a man of the cloth pray for the death of sailors at sea? On the other hand, how could he not pray for his people to prosper? All week he weighed his moral duty against his love for his parishioners.

Still undecided, he mounted the steps of the pulpit on Sunday. The church was full since everyone on the island had heard about the request. He looked down on the rugged, weather-beaten faces of the men and the work-worn hands of the women. After a long pause his voice rose in prayer— "Oh God, if it is thy will that a ship be wrecked, please let it be wrecked on the coast of *our* island!"

The inhabitants of Terschelling, another one of the Wadden Islands, tell the tale of Jouk Haan, a legend which, according to Willem Hoffman, author of *Noord-en Zuidnederlandse Sagen en Legenden*, "touches the soul of the island and coast inhabitants from northern France to Denmark. The men are at home both on the land and on the water . . . but permanently at home on neither."

Jouk Haan felt he belonged to Terschelling. No one knew it better than he. After school he roamed over the eastern end where sand dunes undulated one after the other in an endless row and the sandy beach was so wide that he could run for at least a minute as fast as he could and still not reach the surf. He knew precisely where marsh hens nested in spring, and he watched the fuzzy birdlings waddle in the marram grass. He knew where the big geese stopped in the fall on their way south and where the teals alighted on the little ponds.

Jouk Haan loved the Wadden Sea on the south with its high tides that filled the gullies and low tides that emptied them and the "real" sea on the north, which was strong and powerful.

When he was old enough, he went to sea, first as a deckhand, then as an officer, and later as a captain. He sailed around the world, but no matter what exotic places he visited—China, Ceylon, Japan, Java, or the Caribbean— Jouk Haan longed for his island. When he was on his island, he longed for the sea.

The death of his parents saddened him, and yet it filled him with a guilty joy. Now he could fulfill his dream of buying his own ship with the money received from the sale of their house. He hoped he would feel completely at home on the sea when a ship was his.

Jouk's ship was strong and sturdy. The sailors were the pick of Terschelling's youth. But on the very first voyage, far from home, the sea almost capsized the ship and swallowed its cargo. Was the sea angry because part of his heart still belonged to the island?

On the long way back Jouk pondered where his heart lay. He loved Terschelling, but he would not give up the sea. One day he made his choice and sadly told the sea, "Never, never again shall I feel affection for my island."

From the water below came mocking laughter. Seven mermaids, their silver hair fanned out over the waves, lifted their heads and chanted, "Jouk Haan, Jouk Haan, you will never be able to keep such a promise," and submerged out of sight.

Jouk rebuilt his battered boat, and for many years he did well. He was always glad to see the fire of the Brandaris lighthouse on Terschelling, but not sorry to leave again when he had stashed away his treasures. The islanders shook their heads. What was the use of all his wealth? Here he was, almost forty years old, and he did not have a wife or children to love.

When Jouk decided to equip seven ships for a long and adventurous voyage, he stayed longer on the island than usual to supervise the hammering of joists, the sewing of sails, and the tarring of wood. It was then that he fell deeply in love with a ship captain's daughter and asked her to marry him.

Jouk Haan built a house as far away from the port as possible. He would not leave his bride or ever return to the sea. The mermaids laughed once more on his wedding night, but they were too far away for Jouk Haan to hear them. A tidal wave lifted all his seven ships from their anchors and smashed them on the stone pier, where the proud hulls lay in a jumbled pile. The same great wave took his house and tore Jouk Haan from the arms of his bride.

The old captain buried his daughter on the island. The mermaids kept Jouk Haan.

Saint Nicholas greets children in a department store shortly before his feast day on December 6.

CHAPTER 12

THE SAINT FROM SPAIN

ON ONE OF THOSE DREARY Dutch November days when the sky is a leaden gray and the sun never shines, throngs of patient parents and excited children wait along Amsterdam's Damrak.

Down the street rides a bishop on a splendid white horse. His mitre is trimmed with gold, and a rich red cape falls from his shoulders. What a magnificent long white beard he has! In one white-gloved hand he holds a gilded crosier. With the other he waves slowly, benignly at the children. They wave back and shout, *"Sint Nikolaas! Sinterklaas!"*

Parents lift toddlers high so that they, too, can see Saint Nicholas and Peter, his page, who leads the horse. Peter wears a plumed beret rakishly pulled over one ear, a tight-fitting jacket, and short, puffed britches above long stockings, all in bright, contrasting colors.

Saint Nicholas is making his televised official entry into Amsterdam, which heralds the start of the Sinterklaas season. The mayor and other dignitaries met his ship at the dock while the children sang—

Look, there is the steamer from faraway lands,
It brings us Saint Nicholas, he's waving his hand.
His horse is a-prancing on deck up and down,
The banners are waving in village and town.

Dutch flags are flying from the houses along the saint's

route. He is followed by a brass band, children's organizations, and floats with Cinderella, Sleeping Beauty, Donald Duck, and the Flintstones. Boys who look like Peter are running around with big sacks, handing out cookies and little marzipan animals to the children. They're obviously enjoying their volunteer role in medieval costume.

Who are this cleric and his page?

In A.D. 271 a child was born in Asia Minor who became Nicholas, Bishop of Myra. Many were his good deeds. He rescued three innocent youths from the hangman, and gave a dowry to three poor girls so they could marry three nice boys instead of becoming prostitutes. He miraculously revived three boys who had been cut up by an evil butcher and were left pickled in a barrel for seven years.

After he died, Nicholas came from great distances to rescue those who called on him. Walls tumbled to free innocent prisoners, and seas calmed when ships were about to founder. After he was canonized by the Catholic Church, grateful sailors made Nicholas their patron saint.

When Myra fell to the Moslems, Christians dug up Saint Nicholas's bones and carried them to Bari, Italy, some time in the eleventh century. A shrine was built for these holy relics, and Bari became a destination for pilgrimages. Statues of the saint were revered all over Europe. Perhaps to symbolize the purses with gold coins he gave to the poor maidens, three golden balls were often pictured with him.

Whereas in Russia, Greece, and other countries Nicholas was—and still is—venerated like other saints, fact and fantasy blurred in the Lowlands. There the saint rode a horse through the sky, scattering gifts, just as the pagan god Wodan had done, and like a pagan spirit, he entered people's homes through the chimney. Children put their shoes underneath the flue in the hope that the saint would share his bounty. In convent schools a monk dressed up like a bishop rewarded pupils for good behavior. Gradually, the anniversary of the saint's death on December 6—decreed by the Church as his official calendar day—became a children's feast.

As the wonderful tale of Saint Nicholas was told and retold, his origins became more vague, and finally storytellers had him come from Spain accompanied by a Moorish lad, Peter. Since people in the Lowlands had no idea what Moors looked like, they pictured Peter as dark skinned. The boy who played Peter had his face blackened with soot.

So here we have a Catholic saint doing all those pagan things when the Protestant Reformation came to the Lowlands. The Calvinist burghers bridled. "The Saint Nicholas feast is idolatry," fumed one dominie in a book entitled *Christian Household*. But however much the Calvinists tried to get rid of him, the Catholic saint is still in The Netherlands four hundred years later. He is cherished as the embodiment of gift giving and as a kind of benevolent superman who can vault the barriers of the country's religious and secular factions to unite the Dutch on Sinterklaasavond ("Saint Nicholas Eve") on December 5.

In the weeks that follow the saint's triumphant entry into Amsterdam, children put hay and a carrot in a shoe by the fireplace for his horse and sing,

> Nicholas I beg of you,
> Drop something in my shoe,
> Drop something in my boot.
> Thank you, Dear Sinterklaas.

The next morning their offerings are gone, and in their place is a tangerine or other small gift along with a thank you note that asks what gifts the children would like this year.

There is more to all this than finding and wrapping a gift and hiding it in a closet until the big day. The donor has to write a Sinterklaas poem. Rhymesters in stores will help, but most Dutch struggle with the poems themselves. They often put off this literary chore until Sinterklaasavond, when workers come home a few hours early and the house is full of feverish preparations.

Then someone rings the doorbell, or bangs on the windows, or knocks loudly on the door, or does all three at once. When a child runs to open the door, no one is there. A big sack bulging with gifts lies on the doorstep. Sometimes Sinterklaas sends Peter to stick his black-gloved hand through the living room door and scatter *pepernoten*, baked morsels the size of marshmallows, into the room.

The evening is at its most magical when "Sint" himself pays a visit. He can be hired through a newspaper ad or employment bureau, but it is more fun if Father or Grandpa dresses up in a rented costume. If one of the family is Sinterklaas, he has to give an alibi. "Too bad, I have to go to the garage to have a flat fixed—just now that Saint Nicholas is coming!" he may say.

The saint enters alone or with Peter. After seating himself comfortably in the best chair, he opens a big book, which reminds him to say, "Eva, you should learn to finish your dinner more quickly" or "Martine, it doesn't matter if you lose a game."

Modern views on childrearing have changed Sint's tactics. Not so long ago he made little ones tremble with reproaches like "I hear you're still wetting your bed. Peter will paddle you with his birch rod and put you in his sack if you do it again!" But Peter doesn't walk around with a switch anymore, and children view the sack without fear. It's just a place to put presents.

After praising the youngsters' good habits thoroughly, the venerable visitor leaves. Whoever was Saint Nicholas slips back into the room, and the opening of presents begins.

Everyone reads his or her poem aloud so that others can

share in the humor and gentle teasing. Mother receives a beautifully wrapped package that contains one wrinkled potato along with a poem—

> Here is the poop
> To make some soup.
> When you cut this potato,
> It'll be red like tomato.

Inside, she finds a ring with a red enamel inlay.

As Grandpa opens his box, confetti flies in his face—a spring was cleverly concealed inside. Wouter's package is voluminous. He has to peel off layers of paper, undo knotted strings, and open several tightly taped boxes before he arrives at a minuscule present. Ineke has to search for her gift, following instructions on notes she first has to find.

While the merriment goes on, foot-tall pastry dolls called "lovers" are served along with *boterletter*, fluffy pastry filled with almond paste and shaped into a letter. The children sip hot chocolate, and adults may drink mulled "bishop's wine." A glass is always offered to Sinterklaas who may, if he's the hired kind, swagger over the streets in most unbishoplike fashion after one visit too many.

Relatives and friends leave for their respective homes. The children of the house take their presents to bed, while Father and Mother clean up the paper wrappings. Sinterklaas has gone back to Spain.

Three centuries ago he came with Dutch settlers to the New World. Here he merged with the jolly fat Father Christmas of the English. Without the saint from Spain, there would be no American Santa Claus. That's what comes out when you say "Sinterklaas" quickly.

The "king" of Saint Mauritius Protectors Guild in Limburg in his full regalia. The silver medalions are his symbol of office, which is awarded each year to the marksman who shoots down the king bird.

CHAPTER 13

SHOOTING THE KING BIRD
AND TILTING THE RING

AFTER THE JOYOUS outbursts of merriment and gift giving on Sinterklaasavond, Christmas tends to be a tranquil feast. Families go to church and gather around sumptuous meals featuring roast hare, venison, goose, or turkey. Many homes have a Christmas tree, which is decorated and lit for the first time on Christmas Eve. The candles are often real, necessitating eternal watchfulness and the presence of a bucket of water and stick with a rag behind the tree. In Catholic homes there will probably be a crèche in the living room instead of, or in addition to, the tree. Under pressure from merchants, some families now also exchange presents at Christmastime, but on a more modest scale than at Sinterklaasavond and without the poems and the drolleries.

The lucky Dutch have two Christmas days: First Christmas Day (December 25) and Second Christmas Day (December 26), both national holidays. Second Christmas Day may be the day that the local brass band or choir gives a Christmas concert and citizens have a chance to hear beautiful Dutch Christmas carols with melodies that may date back to the fifteenth century like *Nu Sijt Wellecome, Jesu Lieve Heer* ("Now Be Welcome, Jesus, Dear Lord"). In recent years, community sings around a huge Christmas tree on the town square have become popular.

Here and there older Yuletide traditions remain, like the *midwinterhoornblazen* in Twenthe, Overijssel. To announce the coming of Christ, farmers blow elderwood horns above their wells to amplify the sound, which is passed from farm to farm over the flat, cold landscape.

On New Year's Eve passersby call "*zalig uiteinde*" ("Blessed End") to one another as they hurry home from shops and offices. The whole nation shuts down to celebrate the year's passing. Don't expect to find a taxi or a streetcar after nine o'clock!

I well remember going to church on New Year's Eve and seeing sniffling relatives dab at their noses with handkerchiefs as they sang, "Hours, days, months, years, flee like a shadow." Afterwards, the somber mood lifted when we went to my grandparents' home to play games and munch *oliebollen*, the raisin-studded, deep-fried dough balls that are traditionally served for the event. The grownups had tears in their eyes again when Grootpapa ended the old year by reading Psalm 23 from the family Bible. We youngsters fretted that he wouldn't get through the last verse before midnight and, watching the hand of the big clock standing in the corner, we never heard a word he said.

Grootpapa always timed it right. Just as he solemnly concluded, "I will dwell in the House of the Lord forever," the church bells started to ring, fireworks exploded, and the ships in the harbor blew an off-key tattoo of blasts and toots. Everyone around the big dining room table hugged each other and said, *"Gelukkig nieuwjaar!"* ("Happy New Year").

The first feast of the new year is Epiphany on January 6, celebrated mostly in the Catholic areas by children, who dress up as the three kings or as angels with stars on their heads. Bearing candles, they parade down the streets and sing Epiphany songs like "Here we come with our light/We are looking for the Lord/and welcome the sight."

As Lent approaches, towns in the southern Netherlands

have boisterous carnival revelries, which the Protestant Dutch "above the rivers" don't understand and may look at with a disapproving eye.

Easter brings two days off again: First Easter Day and Second Easter Day. Since Good Friday is often a holiday as well, most Dutch office workers net a four-day weekend. They celebrate Easter variously, depending on their religious bent, but coloring and hunting eggs are usually part of it. In a few rural parts of the country enormous Easter fires are lit. An old belief had it that for as far as the flames were visible, the fields would bear fruit. No one claims this is a Christian tradition, but then, neither is the Christmas tree.

One family feast is observed all over The Netherlands. It is the birthday, a distinctively Dutch celebration.

In the afternoon or evening, those who live close to the *jarige* ("birthday person") drop in to say *"hartelijk gefeliciteerd"* ("Happy Birthday"). The jarige is ready with tea and birthday cake, cookies, and delicious pastries that are often filled with whipped cream. An alternate menu consists of cheese and crackers and round, meat-filled croquettes called *bitterballen*, which are served with wine and Dutch gin.

The guests are seated in a large circle. A new arrival gives the jarige a gift and goes round the circle to shake hands with everyone. When the offspring or parent of the jarige is present, he or she is also congratulated on the happy event.

This kind of party tends to become static. No one moves from his post in the circle unless the host or hostess suggests it, or the guest takes the initiative. Stand-up parties and garden barbecues are winning ground as two of several alternatives for taking care of what is often a virtual army of "drop-ins" for a birthday celebration.

The Dutch remind themselves of birthdays by hanging a birthday calendar in a conspicuous place, usually near the toilet when it is in a separate room from the bath. The calendar has loose pages held together by a string looped through two holes and turned every one or two months. Here dates of birth and death and wedding anniversaries are listed for everyone in the extended family.

The queen's birthday is a national holiday called *koninginnedag* ("queen's day"). Dutch flags fly from government buildings and private homes. Monarchists suspend long orange pennants from the tops of their flagpoles in honor of the House of Orange. Carnivals in town squares across the nation draw merry crowds. When dusk falls, orange lanterns are lit in the trees and electric bulbs in the shape of the first letter of the queen's name light up buildings. Fireworks fill the sky with gorgeous fans and flowers and rivers of colored stars until the displays end with a huge crown-topped initial in honor of the queen.

Juliana's birthday is April 30. Since Beatrix's birthday is on January 31—hardly a good time of year for outdoor celebrations—koninginnedag will continue to be April 30, an appropriate choice since that is the day that Beatrix ascended the throne.

Perhaps the Dutch have created this holiday to make up for the lack of a national independence day. You would think that a nation that fought for eighty years to gain its independence would have an independence day, but there is no such thing. Historians cannot agree on when the Dutch freed themselves from Spanish rule. Was it that day in 1579 when a few provinces decided to unite to fight Spain, or the day in 1580 when the last two of seven provinces signed the Union of Utrecht, or the day in 1648 when a treaty with Spain was finally ratified? By the latter date individual towns had already considered themselves independent for decades. Alkmaar and Leiden, for instance, had been liberated from besieging Spanish troops in 1573 and 1574 respectively, and they remember those dates with their own independence day celebrations. On October 8, everyone in Alkmaar has a half day off and enjoys a big parade. On October 3, Leiden's citizens are served free herring and white bread in remembrance of the food the troops of William of Orange issued to the starving population. In addition, each province has its own folklore events, which draw on its own historic traditions.

Frisians vault over canals and race *skûtsjes*, unwieldy looking flat-bottomed sailing barges with dropboards at the side. The thirteen skûtsjes now in the races are owned by towns or corporations.

Canal vaulting was once an easy way to get from one field to another for agile Frisians who had no time to walk to a bridge. One simply ran towards the canal with a pole in hand, plunged it into the water, and sailed through the air to the opposite side. *Fierljeppen* (Frisian for pole vaulting) has become a sport culminating in an annual tournament held in Winsum. The vaulter no longer runs with the pole in the hand. It is already in the water, and the vaulter sprints over a jetty, grabs the pole, shins as high as he or she can, and, when the swaying pole tilts towards the opposite bank, lets go to fly through the air. If the pole will not lean in the direction of the other bank, it's important to let go of the pole to avoid breaking one's neck on the jetty. Then the vaulter plunges into the water with a big splash as spectators cheer. The record jump to date is 17.84 meters (about fifty-seven feet) with a pole twelve meters (thirty-eight feet) long.

Groningen couples in tilburies pulled by sleek Groninger horses trot smartly around a hippodrome. North Brabant banner-waving guilds execute complicated drills furling and unfurling banners in precision, tossing banners high in the air and catching them.

Drenthe and Gelderland hold sheep-shearing festivals. The purpose is not to find out who can shear the sheep the fastest, but to continue an old tradition of neighborly help at sheep-shearing time. Shearers and onlookers often share a meal. In Ede, Gelderland, it consists of potatoes, salted fish, and butter sauce, and a dessert of *rijstebrij,* rice cooked in milk. In the past these foods were a welcome change from eating bacon all winter and were thought of as well-earned luxuries after the participants had gone from farm to farm to help with the shearing.

Zeeland horses have their feet washed in the sea every spring. This takes place on what was once the island of Schouwen, which is now connected with the rest of The Netherlands by the dams and bridges of the Delta Works. *Strâorien*, as the ritual is called, goes back to pagan times when the sea was thought to expel evil spirits. It was made acceptable to Christians by means of the rationale that horses who had been in the stable all winter should have a chance to stretch their legs. Farmers used to ride their heavy, cream-colored Zeeland draft horses whose huge hooves were hidden in tufts of long, silky hair. They were just the kind of animals needed to pull a plow or a harrow through the sticky Zeeland clay. Now the farmers belong to equestrian clubs and ride saddle horses into the sea in an impressive cavalcade preceded by a music corps.

If you want to see a game of *krulbollen* while you are in Zeeland, you'll have to go to Zeeuwsch-Vlaanderen, just north of the Belgian border, which is the only area in The Netherlands where this ancient pastime is still enjoyed. Men take turns crouching and balancing a *krulbol,* a wooden disk the size of a Gouda cheese, and rolling it with a hefty swing over a sandy course towards a goal pin. *Krul* refers to the "curl" that the asymmetrical disk makes as it spins along.

Better known are the Zeeland ring-tilting contests, which are held on the former islands of Zuid-Beveland and Walcheren. A street in a village or town is roped off and covered with sand.

Suspended from a string between two poles in the center of the course is a ring through which a bareback rider has to thrust a wooden lance while his or her mount travels at a full gallop. A contestant who is lucky enough to ride a husky Zeelander braids its blonde tail and mane with flowers and the national colors.

As the match proceeds, the riders have to aim for ever smaller rings, which may reach the diameter of a wedding ring if the competitors are skillful enough. The winner is "jonah-ed"—grabbed by the arms and legs, tossed several feet into the air, and caught again by the villagers.

For the biggest ring-tilting contest, the one in Middelburg, the white-dressed riders wear orange sashes in honor of the queen, who donated a royal cup for the winner's trophy. In 1978 more than 130 men and women competed for it.

When you travel through the Dutch provinces and come upon a band parading with drums, fifes, and trumpets, followed by men and boys in colorful uniforms, you are probably in Limburg. Gold braids and tassels shine in the sun. Shakos plumed with chicken feathers top the heads of the rank and file while officers sport tall rooster feathers. The left hands of the marchers rest lightly on empty saber sheaths, and right hands firmly grip the hilts of sabers, steel blades pointing upwards from straight arms.

With their weapons and ornate uniforms, the Limburg *schutterijen* recall civic guard paintings, such as *Night Watch* by Rembrandt. Indeed, the Limburg *schutters* ("protectors") were civic guardsmen who protected the local population from overzealous Protestant reformers. Now they protect the cultural heritage as they perpetuate local traditions and old shooting skills.

In 1978, the Guild of Saint Mauritius re-adorned its fifty-odd members with copies of the 1829 gala uniform of the Grenadiers Guard. "It is the best-looking and most expen-

sive uniform ever worn in the Dutch Army," wrote Frans
Ackermans, a lieutenant-colonel of the guild. "It was so
expensive that dear Father State couldn't pay for it and
discontinued the uniform. But what the State could not do, a
Limburg guild could."

Mr. Ackermans' new uniform cost eight hundred dollars,
and the guild had to lay out twenty-five thousand dollars for
the purchase of other members' uniforms. Where did all that
money come from? The guild supplemented its regular
subsidy from the Dutch government by earning money with
fund-raising events and food concessions during shoots and
also elicited contributions from people in the community
who were proud of "their" guild.

Its annual championship shoot is held on the day after
Whitsunday in a meadow beyond which one can see black
and white cows grazing at a safe distance. A forty-five-foot
pole with a bird painted in a circle reaches high into the blue,
cloudless sky.

"To early man the bird was a symbol of power," explained
Mr. Ackermans, " . . . a creature that could fly, walk, and
swim. Games to shoot down a bird fixed to a high point
became popular: the winner felt he gained some of the bird's
power. Limburg guild members shot at a wooden king bird
[so-called because it made the winner king for a year] atop a
tall pole—but the bullets ricocheted off the hard wood and hit
spectators, so we have fixed our king bird on particle board—
it's less authentic, but safer."

In full regalia the Saint Mauritius Guild briskly marches
onto the field. The outgoing king wears the symbol of his
office: the guild's antique, silver-crowned king bird that
hangs from a silver chain around the king's neck. Draped
over his front and back is the "king silver," an "armor" of
fist-size silver shields in oval, round, rectangular, and
escutcheon shapes, linked with more silver chains. Engraved

on the shields are the names of previous kings.

When his turn comes, each schutter doffs his warm woolen coat with the gold trim and his fancy hat, and then props the guild's antique forty-pound rifle on a stand. The one who shoots a hole in the circle gets applause. Lots of holes in the circle eventually bring it and the king bird down, and he who fires the decisive shot is king for a year.

Almost every weekend during spring and summer, a protectors guild has a similar contest somewhere in Limburg. Regional contests follow, and the winning guilds compete in the annual Oud Limburgs Schuttersfeest ("Old Limburg Protectors Festival"). Guilds from both Dutch and Belgian Limburg compete, since the two provinces were joined from 1814 to 1839, when Belgium and The Netherlands were united. One hundred-fifty guilds, each with drummers and trumpeters, join in a parade three miles long. A jury gives prizes to the king who has arranged his king silver in the most artistic way and to the best-dressed queen (a king's wife, sister, or girl friend). The jury also presides over a marching contest in which the guilds are penalized for members who chew gum, wear rundown heels, have spots on their snow-white spats, or commit other breaches of schutter's etiquette.

"A life without feasts is like a road without rest stops," said the ancient Greek philosopher Democritus, and the Dutch have a good many rest stops, several distinctively Dutch.

There are the national ones, like Saint Nicholas Eve and the queen's birthday and those "second" Christmas, Easter, and Whitsun days. There is the intimate birthday party that may pass you by as a visitor if you are not close to a Dutch family. And there are the colorful local festivals where riders on enormous horses spear a tiny ring or men shoot at the figure of a bird on a tall pole. Whether you'll be able to see any of what the tourist brochures call "folkloristic" events depends on when and where you are in The Netherlands.

Father pours coffee, Judy passes the butter, Arja pauses to tell a joke at Sunday *koffietafel* laden with raisin buns, breads, cheeses, cold meats, chocolate paste, and sprinkles.

CHAPTER 14

HUSSAR SALAD AND HUNTER'S DISH

CALORIE WATCHERS, beware of sharing meals with the Dutch. A home-cooked Dutch meal is delicious, but bread is the basis for breakfast and luncheon menus, potatoes are almost always served at dinnertime, and the Dutch love to snack in between.

Breakfast consists of *boterhammen*, buttered slices of bread with something on top. There is usually a selection of bread and a choice of toppings like jam, cheese, and sliced cold meat. There may be fruit juice and a soft-boiled egg in a cup with a bonnet. Tea or coffee complement the first meal of the day.

At mid-morning coffee is made in the Dutch way. It's strong, percolated, and diluted with thick "coffee milk." For special occasions the beverage may be accompanied by a *saucijzenbroodje*—a flaky pastry roll with a sausage inside—or a sweet pastry.

Lunch is an elaborate version of breakfast called *koffietafel* ("coffee table") because coffee is generally served. The more festive a hostess wants the koffietafel to be, the more toppings she is likely to serve and the greater the choice of breads. Sometimes the table seems buried beneath its load of platters and dishes, jars and bowls. The bread basket is the center of attention, and it holds a variety of sliced breads: whole wheat, white, raisin bread, and the blackest rye you ever saw. Round *beschuit*, known to Americans as Holland Rusk, and

slices of spiced bread called *ontbijtkoek* or *koek* are also
served. Wedges of cheese rest under a glass dome, and
platters display paper-thin smoked beef, roast beef, veal,
sausage, herring, and smoked eel. There are sliced raw
vegetables like tomatoes and cucumbers along with straw-
berries in season. Sweets include the expected jam and
honey as well as chocolate sprinkles called *hagelslag*,
colorful anise-flavored morsels called *muisjes* ("little mice"),
and spicy cookies known as *speculaas*.

Each person takes one piece of bread, spreads it with
butter, and helps himself to one kind of topping. Stacking is
frowned upon as being unnecessary. A *houtsnip* ("wood-
cock"), a white boterham with cheese and black rye on top, is
permissible, however, and *speculaas* may be laid two abreast
on white *boterham*.

How are you going to sample everything on the table if you
have to eat an entire boterham with only one topping? You
must consume at least a dozen slices of bread unless your
hostess suggests that you throw Dutch etiquette to the winds
and cut a slice of buttered bread into pieces so that you may
decorate each piece with a different topping. Then you have
what is called a *volkstuintje* after the "little gardens for the
people" that municipal authorities allocate on the outskirts
of town to apartment dwellers. These gardens are often
colorful and varied.

Your Dutch table neighbor may eat the boterham with
knife and fork, cutting off one piece at a time and bringing it to
the mouth with the fork. He or she doesn't lay down the knife
before each bite as is the American custom. When the Dutch
are not eating, both hands lie on the table, wrists at table's
edge. "I don't see both your hands," a Dutch mother says to
her children, just as an American parent says, "Take that
hand off the table, please."

You'll find the koffietafel a pleasant meal with lots of

"Please pass me the —" and "May I serve you some—" as bread, butter, and toppings are passed around the table. But if you are used to eating cottage cheese and a pear for lunch, the koffietafel may offer too much food for your comfort, particularly if you are invited to another home for tea on the same day. A Dutch tea is not by any means as elaborate as English tea, but the fresh cookies, often baked with lots of butter, and rich pastry may easily turn a tea into another meal.

Tea rituals seem to vary little. At four o'clock, relatives and neighbors drop in to share the latest news. The participants sit in a circle, and every time someone joins the group or leaves it, he or she makes the rounds to shake hands. In some homes strict rules determine who gets up from his or her seat for the handshaking. A woman rises for another woman the same age, for instance, but not for a woman much younger. A foreign visitor passing through The Netherlands will not be expected to know these intricacies.

If you are the subject of an impromptu dinner invitation after tea, you are in luck. Had the hostess known you were coming, she might have prepared something fancy, like Spanish paella or cheese fondue. As it is, you will have real Dutch food. "Have you eaten warm?" she may ask, since the Dutch may have their hot meal of the day either at noon or in the evening.

Dutch food is wholesome and hearty. A warm meal may start with a soup served in a large plate with a rim and eaten with a spoon so big that Americans would call it a serving spoon. Next come potatoes, meat or fish, and vegetables. The meat will most likely be served with gravy made from the drippings in the meat pan to which a generous dollop of butter was added. The vegetables will probably be fresh. After all, in a little land where the farthest market garden is but a few hours away from the auction hall and the retail store, there is no need for days or weeks of refrigerated storage.

In some rural parts of the country, the Dutch still eat potatoes as the potato eaters in Vincent van Gogh's painting of the same name did, with a fork from a large pot in the center of the table. Today's potato eaters do not look haggard as did van Gogh's peasants, however, and they have other nourishing foods to eat along with the potatoes.

Popular varieties are Eigenheimers, Bintjes, Blauwpiepers, and the tiny new potatoes that are harvested in the spring. All of them are sold peeled in plastic bags. The purchaser takes the potatoes home and puts them in water until it's time to cook them for the warm meal. Chances are that you will eat "crumb potatoes," which are boiled with so little water that it has evaporated by the time the potatoes are cooked. The pan is then shaken, and "crumbs" come off the potatoes.

Certain fruits and vegetables tend to accompany favorite main dishes. A serving of homemade apple sauce in many homes belongs with fried chicken, as does a serving of stewed pears that naturally take on a deep rose color during cooking or have the help of a dash of red currant juice. Mashed potatoes are preferred over regular potatoes with boiled tongue and sour sauce. Baby carrots or carrots and peas are served with fish.

Dessert may be a pudding or fresh fruit topped with yogurt or *kwark*, a cottage-type cheese.

At the table you'll note certain differences from home. If you are a houseguest, the cloth envelope next to your plate is provided for your napkin rather than a napkin ring. The knife rest is used for your knife between courses. Some people eat fish with a fish knife and fork. Water without ice will be served with the meal unless there is cold beer or wine.

Before the meal you may be served sherry or potent Dutch gin in tiny glasses although mixed drinks and whiskeys are now gaining ground. After dinner the teapot may reappear with, yes, more cookies.

Visitors to The Netherlands have been disappointed in the fact that it is difficult to find typical Dutch foods in restaurants. The elaborate *koffietafel* is served rarely now because labor costs in preparation and the waste of leftover cut meats make it an expensive production on a commercial basis. There are, however, many quick-service *broodjeswinkels* ("bread shops"), where you can order an open-faced sandwich topped with a mountain of thinly sliced meat or a sausage of your choice from a bewildering array on the counter.

You can also find Dutch specialties at fairs, country markets, and that festive annual institution, the town *braderie*, when merchants take over a street to exhibit their wares and craftsmen demonstrate their skills. At these events you may see a man making small, crisp waffles known as *stroopwafels* with a special iron or mini-pancakes called *poffertjes*, which are made in batches of sixty-four at once in a huge cast-iron pan.

A few old-fashioned *poffertjes* tent restaurants still move from fair to fair. Their sculpted woodwork is gaily painted like a barrel organ, and inside, glass chandeliers hang from the ceiling and mirrors to make the pavilion seem bigger. One such antique restaurant is stationed permanently in The Hague at the Old Market near the Houses of Parliament. Other permanent ones, all likely to be open the better part of the year, include tents in Rotterdam and, close to Hilversum, in Bussum and Laren. The latter is particularly fanciful.

Herring stalls appear in the spring when the herring boats come in with their first catch of the season—a happy event that was once announced by little flags on the streetcars of fishing towns. "Green" herring is eaten just as it comes from the sea. After a few weeks, when the fish have lost the greenness of their youth, "new" herring is still eaten raw but salted. You may have seen photos of the Dutch eating raw herring by grabbing the little fish by the tail, throwing their heads back, and dropping in the delicacy. Many Dutch prefer to eat theirs from a paper plate or on a boterham provided by the herring vendor.

Some specialties that originated in other countries are now as Dutch as poffertjes and herring. Numerous stalls sell *patates frites*, a treat borrowed from the Belgians. Mounds of French-fried potatoes topped with mayonnaise are served in a cone-shaped bag along with a wooden stick for spearing. Patates are popular with the young, who now spend their pocket money on them instead of chocolate bars. From the Far East come such snacks as Chinese *loempia*, a little folded pancake that is filled with vegetables and deep fried, and Indonesian *sateh*, small pieces of roasted meat on a skewer which are dipped in a spicy peanut sauce.

As for foreign restaurants, you will find all the kinds you find at home, from French *haute cuisine* to American fast food chains selling hamburgers and fried chicken.

Indonesian restaurants are common, and one of their specialties may provide the greatest dining adventure in The Netherlands today. It is the *rijsttafel* ("rice table"), a leftover from the days when returning colonists longed for foods they had enjoyed in Java and Sumatra.

The traditional rijsttafel, a meal of rice and a multitude of side dishes, was brought to the table by a procession of white-clad waiters, sometimes as many as twenty, each bearing one dish. Their heads were covered with a folded cloth to fulfill the Moslem requirement that a man should cover his head, and the pattern and design of this batik head covering indicated the region they were from. Now the waiters are not always Indonesians and their heads are mostly bare, but the number of dishes is the same. There are vegetables in coconut milk, vegetables and sateh with peanut sauce, meatballs in saffron sauce, fried bananas, and fish and chicken prepared in various ways. Certainly there are *kroepoek*, small chips of dried shrimp paste that puff to many times their original size when fried in very hot oil. A word of caution is in order regarding the *sambal*, peppery hot ground red chilies. Take a portion no larger than the tip of your knife since no amount of beer or water will soothe your palate or the inside of your pharynx if you are not used to the fiery stuff.

You may have to ask the waiter in a Dutch restaurant for your check since he probably will not bring it with the dessert. The tips are included in the bill, but after dinner coffee is an extra charge. It is served in a demitasse and strong. Drinking large cups of weaker coffee with the meal is not a Dutch custom.

Whether you dine in homes or in restaurants or help yourself to the offerings of outdoor food vendors, you will find Dutch food to be fresh and tasty. To alleviate the effects of the caloric intake, perhaps you can do what a friend of mine does during his visits to The Netherlands. He locates the nearest exercise course. (There are at least two hundred of them in The Netherlands, and every town has at least one.) Then, between invitations to Dutch homes, indulgences at poffertjes stands, and sumptuous restaurant meals, he leaps over hurdles and touches his toes, as instructed by the signs along the course.

If you would like to sample Dutch cooking in your own home, pick and choose from among the following recipes. They are the kind that anyone who grew up in The Netherlands is likely to remember, perhaps with nostalgia, as being "typically Dutch."

Huzarensla ("Hussar Salad")

You don't see mounted hussars in colorful uniforms anymore, but presumably they had hearty appetites that could be satisfied with this meal-in-one salad. It can easily be made a day or so ahead. Take the salad out of the refrigerator before serving since it tastes better when not ice cold.

 1 pound cold meat, diced
 3 green sour apples, unpeeled, cored, and diced
 3 hard-boiled eggs, chopped
 1 cooked beet, diced (or 1 16-ounce can diced beets, drained)
 6 boiled potatoes, mashed coarsely while hot
 4 dill pickles, sliced
10 or more small pickled onions
 3 tablespoons oil
 3 tablespoons vinegar
 ½ teaspoon salt
 ¼ teaspoon pepper

Let potatoes cool. Combine all ingredients. Put the salad on a platter and shape it into any form you wish. Spread it with mayonnaise and decorate with slices of pickle, parsley sprigs, and tomato.
Serves 8.

Croquetten

Breaded "sausages" filled with creamed meat are deep fried and served on boterhammen.

 ½ pound lean meat
 1 small onion
 1 bay leaf
 2 eggs, separated
 2 tablespoons butter or margarine
 3 tablespoons flour
 1 teaspoon lemon juice
 ½ teaspoon salt
 ¼ teaspoon pepper (or ½ teaspoon curry powder)
Bread crumbs
Oil for deep frying
Parsley (optional)

Simmer meat with salt, onion, and bay leaf in 1½ cups water until meat is well done (at least 1 hour). Save and strain the stock. Measure it, adding water if necessary, to equal 1 cup. Cut meat into very small pieces. Melt butter in saucepan and blend in flour. Blend stock with butter-flour mixture. Bring to boil over medium heat, and cook until thickened, stirring constantly. Remove from heat and add the lemon juice, the pepper or curry powder, and the two beaten egg yolks, as well as the meat. Spread the mixture in a shallow dish. Cover and chill until firm, at least 2 hours or as long as overnight. Cut into ten equal parts and, with floured hands, roll into firm cylinders. Roll them in bread crumbs. Dip the croquettes in a mixture of the 2 egg whites and 2 tablespoons of water placed in a bowl. Then roll them through bread crumbs again. Be sure they are well coated on all sides. Deep fry in hot oil (400° F.) until chestnut brown. Drain and serve hot, garnished with sprigs of parsley that have been fried just until crisp in the oil. To reheat, bake uncovered in a 375° oven until hot, about 20 minutes. This recipe yields ten croquettes about 3 inches long and 1 inch in diameter.

One cup diced, cooked chicken or cooked shrimp may be substituted for the meat.

To make *bitterballen*, which are served as appetizers, shape the mixture into balls about 1 inch in diameter. Serve hot with toothpicks.

Whether round or sausage shaped, *croquetten* are served with mustard.

Makes 10

Uitsmijter ("Throw-Outer")

This boterham used to be served at the end of an evening party. The appearance of the uitsmijter meant, "The fun is over, and we're throwing you out." Now the dish is a favorite quick meal in a restaurant, where you can ask for a *hele uitsmijter* (two pieces of bread) or a *halve uitsmijter* (one slice of bread). You may specify how you would like your egg cooked, and what kinds of bread and meat or cheese you want. To make half an uitsmijter at home you need:

  1 slice of bread of your choice
     Butter or margarine
     Thinly sliced roast beef, veal, ham, or cheese
  1 egg
     Salt and pepper

Butter the bread, and place thin slices of meat on top. The Dutch often "drape" the meat over the boterham so it falls like a skirt on the plate. Fry an egg to your liking and place on top of meat. Season with salt and pepper.

Vermicellisoep met balletjes
("Vermicelli Soup with Little Meatballs")

Soup: 4 cups clear beef stock
         ½ cup vermicelli, broken into 1-inch pieces
         ½ teaspoon salt
         ¼ teaspoon marjoram or a blade of mace

Meatballs: 1 or 2 slices of white bread
                Milk
             ½ pound ground beef or veal
             1 egg, beaten
             ¼ teaspoon grated nutmeg
             ¼ teaspoon salt

Trim the crusts from the bread and soak in just enough milk to moisten thoroughly. Combine with the rest of the ingredients for meatballs. Shape into balls about ½ to ¾ inch in diameter and set aside. Bring the stock to a boil with salt and mace or marjoram. Add the vermicelli and cook for time specified on

package. Add meatballs for the last 10 minutes of cooking time.
Serves 6.

Erwtensoep ("Pea Soup")

This is a winter soup. When ice is on the Dutch canals, vendors sell it steaming hot to skaters. Some people claim that you should make the soup a day ahead since it tastes better warmed up. Add more vegetables or potatoes if you wish, or go easy on the meat. Dutch recipes usually call for pig's feet, but ham hocks are a good substitute.

2   cups split peas (12-ounce package), soaked in water
      overnight
8   cups water
2   pounds ham hocks
1   large onion, cut up
4   leeks, cut up
3   celery stalks, cut up
1   12-ounce package smoked sausage links, sliced
1   teaspoon thyme
1   teaspoon salt
½   teaspoon pepper
4   to 6 potatoes, diced (optional)

Simmer peas and ham hocks in water in a covered pot for 2 hours (preferably a cast-iron pot). Remove the meat from the bones and return the meat to the pot. Add the seasonings, cut-up vegetables, smoked sausage, and the potatoes if you use them. Simmer for at least another hour. Some cooks say the soup has to be simmered much longer. That's fine, as long as you check the pot often to make sure the soup isn't sticking to it.
Serves 6.

Stamppot van boerenkool met worst
Kale, Potato, and Sausage

The plant with the big green leaves that Americans call kale is known as *boerenkool* ("farmer's cabbage") in The Netherlands. "Boerenkool is best when taken from the ground after the frost has gone over it," say the Dutch. If they cook kale before the first frost, they put it in the crisper for a day or so. The meat that the Dutch serve with the *stamppot* (literally, "mashing pot") is Gelderland *rookworst*, a smoked sausage that is rarely available abroad. Substitute Polish sausage or smoked sausage links.

2   to 3 pounds kale
3   pounds potatoes, cut up
¼   cup fat (lard or bacon drippings)
1   teaspoon salt
1   pound sausage

Strip the kale leaves from the stalks and discard stalks. Wash leaves and boil in small amount of water for 1 hour. Drain leaves and mince. Put the potatoes in a big pot and add the salt and about half the amount of water needed to cover them. Layer the kale on top and dot with fat. Cover and cook slowly until the water has boiled away, about 30 minutes. Add small amount of stock or milk to prevent burning if the water boils away before the potatoes are cooked. Mash with a potato masher and serve with sausage.
Serves 6.

Hutspot

Carrot and Potato Stew

The people of Leiden eat *hutspot* on October 3 to commemorate the town's liberation by Prince William of Orange in 1574. Leiden had been under siege for several months, and the townspeople were starving. Then Prince William ordered the sluices opened to flood the surrounding land, and the besieging Spaniards retreated. When a Leiden boy climbed up to explore the deserted ramparts, he found a big black iron pot with a stew containing beef and vegetables. Except for the addition of potatoes, this hutspot is a close copy.

The Dutch make hutspot with *klapstuk*, boneless beef short ribs, which are not usually available in American markets. If you cannot have the beef cut to order, cook the stew without the meat and serve sausage with it.

2   pounds boneless short ribs
2   to 4 pounds carrots, sliced
4   pounds potatoes, diced
2   large onions, chopped
4   tablespoons fat, butter, or margarine
    Salt and pepper

Simmer the meat in 2 cups salted water for about 2 hours. Take out the meat and keep warm in a covered pot. Add potatoes, carrots, and onion to the liquid. Simmer until the vegetables are cooked, adding more liquid if necessary, and until excess moisture has evaporated. Mash the mixture with a potato masher, season with salt and pepper, and serve with chunks of the reserved meat.
Serves 6.

Jachtschotel ("Hunter's Dish")

In the past, this dish was made with leftover venison, but few Dutch eat venison anymore. For that matter, few may have leftover meat. To start from scratch, you'll need:

1   pound lean stewing beef
3   onions, sliced very thin
2   large tart apples, sliced and peeled
12 medium-sized potatoes, boiled and mashed

> 2 tablespoons butter
> 1 tablespoon Worcestershire sauce
> ¼ teaspoon nutmeg
> ½ teaspoon salt
> ¼ teaspoon pepper
>   Bread crumbs

Remove membranes and fat from the meat and cut into small pieces. Saute onions in butter until transparent and add the meat and brown. Add seasonings, Worcestershire sauce, and 1 cup water, and let simmer in covered pot until meat is tender, at least 1 hour. Meanwhile, boil the potatoes and mash them. Salt to taste. In a buttered, ovenproof dish, place *half* the mashed potatoes, add the stew, and top with apple slices. Cover with the other half of the mashed potatoes. Sprinkle bread crumbs on top and dot with butter. Bake for 30 minutes in a moderate oven (350°). If you assemble the dish a day ahead, bake for at least 1 hour, particularly if you use a heavy casserole.

Red cabbage is a good accompaniment for jachtschotel. *Serves 6.*

Spinazie met soldaatjes

("Spinach with Little Soldiers")

The Dutch prepare their vegetables not too differently from Americans or Canadians, but the following recipe has a definite "Dutch touch."

> 3 packages frozen chopped spinach cooked until tender
> 6 tablespoons butter
> 3 slices white bread, cut into strips
> 3 hard-boiled eggs, quartered

Add 3 tablespoons butter to the cooked spinach and keep warm in the oven. In a separate pan, fry the strips of bread in

the remaining butter and place the "little soldiers" upright in the spinach just before serving. The quartered eggs go between the little soldiers.
Serves 6.

Stoofpeertjes
("Little Stewing Pears")

These are the pears the Dutch like to eat warm or cold with fowl. The Dutch stewing variety gets dark pink because of its nature or the addition of red currant sauce, but any pear you stew will turn pink, too, because of the red wine.

1 cup water
1 cup dry red wine
1 cup sugar
12 pears, peeled, cored, and quartered
2 cinnamon sticks
½ teaspoon grated lemon rind

Bring water, wine, and sugar to a boil and cook, stirring constantly, until sugar is dissolved. Add pears and simmer until almost tender. Add cinnamon and lemon rind and continue simmering until pears are cooked through.
Serves 12.

Broodschoteltje met sinaasappels
("Bread Dish with Oranges")

Dutch cookbooks are full of recipes for hot and cold puddings for those who don't want to buy dessert in a carton from the milkman. Here is one of them that is just right for serving on a snowy winter evening.

8 slices white bread without crusts
2 cups fresh orange juice
½ cup butter, softened

¾ cup sugar
2 eggs, separated
   Grated rind of ½ lemon

Mash bread with orange juice until mixture is very smooth
(preferably in an electric blender). Cream butter with sugar
until light and fluffy. Stir in egg yolks and lemon rind, and
beat until mixture is light and creamy. Mix into bread
mixture. Fold in egg whites beaten to soft peaks. (For a fluf-
fier dessert, add the beaten whites of two more eggs.) Bake
in greased 1½-quart casserole at 325° for 1 hour.
Serves 6.

Poffertjes ("Little Puffy Pancakes")

These are the same treats you buy at poffertjes stalls at fairs
or in those crystal-chandeliered, mirrored pavilions. In The
Netherlands you can buy a poffertjes pan, a griddle with
depressions, but you can make the poffertjes equally well in
any frying pan.

1   package active dry yeast
¼ cup warm water (about 110°)
2   tablespoons sugar
1   cup milk
1   egg, beaten
¼ teaspoon nutmeg
½ teaspoon salt
1¾ cups all-purpose flour
    Melted butter
    Powdered sugar

Dissolve the yeast in warm water and blend in the sugar,
milk, egg, nutmeg, salt, and flour. Cover and let rise for 45
minutes. Heat a large frying pan over medium heat. Lightly
brush pan with melted butter, or let butter swirl over the
surface of the pan until it is entirely covered. Spoon level

tablespoonsful of batter into the pan so that poffertjes do not touch. Bake them until lightly browned on bottom side; turn and bake on other side until browned. Serve with soft butter and powdered sugar.
Serves 6 to 10.

Ontbijtkoek ("Breakfast Cake")

You don't have to eat this spiced cake for breakfast or on a boterham as described for the koffietafel. A slice of *koek* is also eaten on its own, spread with butter. Each Dutch province and some towns have their own special recipes for koek, which are closely guarded by the local bakers. The following recipe is enhanced by the use of crystallized ginger.

2 cups self-rising flour
½ cup dark brown sugar
⅓ cup molasses
1 cup milk
1 teaspoon ground cloves
1 teaspoon ground ginger
1 teaspoon ground cinnamon
½ teaspoon ground nutmeg
¼ teaspoon salt
   Crystallized ginger, chopped (optional)

Combine all ingredients into a smooth paste. (If you use crystallized ginger, chop up about five pieces, each walnut size.) Butter a 4½x8½-inch loaf pan. Fill with dough and bake for about 1 hour in a 300° oven. The koek is done when a knife inserted near the center comes out clean. To prevent the nicely risen koek from collapsing after baking, let it cool off in the oven with the temperature turned off and the door open.

   The Dutch keep koek in the breadbin to retain moisture. Wrap it well if you store it in the refrigerator.

Roggebrood ("Rye Bread")

The Dutch rye bread is rectangular and black. This easy-to-make substitute will be round and brown, but the taste is close to the Dutch variety. Many "natural food" stores in the United States have bins with bran and rye flour so that you can buy just as much as you need.

    2½ cups wheat bran
    1½ cups rye flour
     ⅓ cup black molasses
     1 teaspoon salt
    1½ cups boiling water

Combine ingredients and pack tightly into a 1-pound coffee can. Put the lid on the can and steam 1½ hours in a covered pan of boiling water. Let the roggebrood cool slightly, uncovered, and invert onto a rack. Do not cut while the bread is still warm. Eat buttered with cheese, white sugar, or *stroop*, a heavy sugar syrup that you may find in import stores. Stroop tastes much the same as English treacle.

Speculaas

In The Netherlands these spiced cookies are sold in packages or by the pound. In the past, they were made on *koekplanken* ("cookie planks"), which were boards imprinted with the shapes of windmills, mermaids, and elephants. You can still find koekplanken in antique stores, but modern copies may be made only for wall decoration. Today's speculaas are made to resemble the handmade kind of yesteryear and are usually in a windmill pattern.

    1 cup white sugar
    1 cup brown sugar
    1 cup butter or margarine, softened
    2 eggs, beaten

> 2 teaspoons vanilla
> 3½ cups flour
> 2 teaspoons baking soda
> ¼ teaspoon ground cloves
> ¼ teaspoon allspice
> 1 teaspoon cinnamon
> 1 teaspoon nutmeg
> ⅛ teaspoon salt

Cream the sugars with the butter and vanilla. Blend in the beaten eggs and beat well. Sift the flour with the rest of the dry ingredients and beat into the butter mixture. Divide dough into 2 equal portions and shape into long, oval-shaped rolls, about 2½ by 1½ inches in diameter. Wrap in waxed paper or foil and chill in refrigerator overnight. Cut into ⅛- or ¼-inch slices and place ½ inch apart on a greased cookie sheet. Bake in preheated 350° oven 10 to 15 minutes, depending on the thickness of the cookies. The thin cookies will be crisp, and the thicker ones a bit chewy.
Makes at least 6 dozen cookies.

Boterletter

The letters that are given away on Saint Nicholas Eve are available in all Dutch pastry shops during the holiday season although you may have to order your letter ahead. Traditional Dutch recipes call for old-fashioned puff pastry, the kind you roll, fold, chill, roll, and fold as described in any standard American cookbook. Here is a shortcut that's far less tedious and produces a respectable, even if not 100-percent authentic, puff pastry.

If you only have unblanched almonds, remove the skins by scalding them in hot water and rubbing them against each other with your fingers. Make the filling several weeks ahead.
Filling:
> ¼ pound blanched almonds

½ cup sugar
1 egg, beaten
Pinch of salt
Grated rind of 1 lemon

Dough:
1 cup cold butter (do not use margarine)
2 cups all-purpose flour
½ cup sour cream
1 egg yolk, beaten

Grind the almonds in a meat grinder or food processor. Mix with sugar, beaten egg, lemon peel, and salt. Grind the entire mixture again. Keep well-wrapped in refrigerator. Before you need the paste, roll it into sausages about 1 inch in diameter.

To make the dough, cut up the butter into ½-inch cubes. Combine with the flour, cutting butter into the flour with a pastry blender or two knives until butter particles are about the size of peas. Mix the sour cream with the egg yolk and add to the butter and flour mixture, blending with a fork until you obtain a clinging "dough ball." Separate the ball into two portions and chill, well-wrapped, in refrigerator for several hours or days. When you take dough out of refrigerator, allow time for it to reach room temperature. (If your kitchen is warm, butter dough may start to melt: chill dough again until firm.)

Roll the dough ⅛ inch thick on wax paper or floured surface. Cut into strips 3½ inches wide. Place the almond paste sausages end to end along the center, fold dough over them, and seal top and ends with water. Leave dough as a bar or shape into a letter. Place seam down on a cookie sheet greased with unsalted shortening. Brush with beaten egg diluted with water. Bake at 400° for 20 minutes, or until golden brown.

At Christmas time the Dutch turn the boterletter into a *kerstkrans* ("Christmas wreath"). Shape a ring instead of a letter. Spread with confectioner's icing while the pastry is still hot and decorate with candied cherries, orange and lemon peel, and a red bow.

Bisschopwijn ("Bishop's Wine")

This favorite holiday drink may have been named after Saint Nicholas, once the bishop of Myra.

15 cloves
1 orange
1 lemon
½ cup sugar
1 whole nutmeg
1 stick cinnamon
2 to 4 cups apple cider or apple juice
2 bottles red wine such as claret or Burgundy

Make small incisions in orange and lemon and insert the cloves. Dissolve the sugar in 2 cups boiling apple cider and add with the cinnamon and nutmeg to the wine. Let wine steep with the fruit in a covered pot over a very slow fire. Do not boil.

The Dutch toast each other with "*Gezondheid*" ("Your Health") or "*Proost*," which means the same. Some not only look deeply into your eyes as they lift their glasses and pronounce the salutation, but again, after savoring a sip, as they put their glasses down.

A pewterer in Rotterdam's House of the Sack Carriers puts the finishing touch to beakers made from ancient molds.

CHAPTER 15

POTTERY, PEWTER, AND PENDULUM CLOCKS

IF YOU WANT to know what Dutch craftsmen made for the home long ago, you'll find answers in the paintings of the seventeenth-century masters. Pewter mugs, willow baskets, earthenware jugs, and decorated tiles are shown with careful detail in charming domestic scenes.

To find out what craftsmen make today, go to a Dutch department store that sells some "typically Dutch" items or a tourist shop, where they're all assembled for your convenience. Many shapes and designs have not changed since the days of Rembrandt and Vermeer!

Dutch tiles in blue, red, and many-colored polychrome are still hand painted with tulips, drawbridges, mermaids, and sailing ships. Once they were applied to entire walls and fireplaces with a lavish touch, but handmade tiles are now so costly that they are used sparingly. You'll see them grouted together in sets of six or nine as tops for small tables or grouped on a living room wall, each tile in its own frame. They add a colorful accent to a kitchen when they are lined up in a gay stripe above the counter or randomly placed among plain tiles that cover a wall.

Delftware—a variety of blue and other monotone as well as polychrome vases, bowls, and plates—has an unexpected non-European look. The designs feature exotic birds and oriental scenes borrowed from the Chinese wares that Dutch seafarers brought home from their travels. The town of Delft in the province of Holland once sheltered a colony of potters, but now only one pottery is left: the Royal Delft Earthenware Factory, which has earned the title "royal" for its excellence in craftsmanship. Also known as De Porceleyne Fles ("The Porcelain Jar"), Royal Delft signs all its pieces with a jar, the initials JT after an early partner named Joost Thooft, and the word "Delft."

Shoppers after the genuine article should beware of pieces not made by hand and maybe not even made in The Netherlands. Besides De Porceleyne Fles, only one other large Dutch firm makes pottery in the traditional way. It is called Makkumware after a tiny Frisian town on the border of Lake IJssel. Here ten generations of the family Tichelaar, which means "tile maker," have owned the Royal Tichelaar Earthenware Factory. Their pieces are signed with crossed *T*s and the word "Makkum."

Good-natured rivalry exists between the two royal potteries. Which is the oldest? "The Jar" dates from 1653, while Makkum celebrated its "official" three-hundredth anniversary in 1960. (Dishes and tiles have been unearthed that may prove the factory existed before 1660.)

Spokesmen for Delft claim their bright blue is best, and advocates for Makkum insist their subdued blue is more beautiful. Delft is proud of its new jet black pottery painted with traditional motifs, and Makkum vaunts its new oven-proof dinnerware of modern design, done in soft tones of brown and green that are plucked right out of the Dutch landscape.

The two potteries produce their time-honored wares in almost the same way. An artisan throws a form on a wheel or casts it in a plaster mold and then bisque fires the result in a kiln. Another artisan transfers the design with powdered charcoal or pumice and a perforated paper stencil and then paints in the colors with a brush made from the hairs of the inside of a cow's ear. The piece is then fired for the second time. The only difference between the Makkum and Delft processes is the clay they use. Delft imports white clay and applies a transparent glaze before the second firing. Makkum uses reddish Friesland clay and coats it with a white tin oxide glaze after the first firing; no glaze is necessary for the second firing.

Both firms manufacture wall plates with the sayings the Dutch are so fond of, like "A good start is half the work" and "Who perseveres, wins." They also accept orders for commemorative plates. One of the Delft's several choices for a wedding plate shows a couple at the helm of a flat bottom sailing boat. A dog next to them symbolizes faith, and in the sail are two rings. The waves below make room for the names of bride and groom and the wedding date.

A few miles south of Makkum in the little town of Workum, a much more rugged-looking earthenware is manufactured in three potteries.

Workum's farmer's pottery, known in the trade as "slipware," comes in an earthy rust. Its only decoration is a wavy, cream-colored line of slip that used to be applied with a sawed-off cow horn but now is squirted from a plastic bottle. A popular slipware jug seems to have walked right out of Vermeer's famous painting, *The Kitchen Maid*. If you buy one, be sure to ask if the glaze is lead-free if you intend to use it for milk as Vermeer's maid did.

On the table in Vermeer's painting there is a willow breadbasket that is still being copied today. The making of willow baskets, cradles, and chairs used to be a home industry that kept hundreds of craftsmen busy. Willow twigs are still plentiful, but the basket braiders are disappearing. You may have to search a bit for a "Vermeer" breadbasket in Dutch basket shops, and you may find that the baskets there are imported from Yugoslavia, Korea, and China.

A truly Dutch item that you may find in such stores is a ladder-back chair with a seat of woven rushes that had their origin in a placid Dutch river. The Brabant knob chair, a model that has been around since long before the Golden Age, has hand-carved round knobs atop its four-rung ladder. In several parts of The Netherlands, artisans used to paint such chairs and decorate them with garlands or biblical scenes set in a medalion. Only Hindeloopers in Friesland still practice this old art. They brush age-old patterns of bows, flowers, and luck-bringing birds of paradise over tones of deep red or green—and sometimes white or blue—on a variety of wood objects ranging from furniture to napkin rings. As with Dutch pottery, these now traditional designs were once borrowed from foreign lands. In this instance, local captains brought them home from the Baltic states, which they visited when Hindeloopen was a prospering port.

Dutch seafarers brought home more than just decorating ideas. From South America they brought copper for the lidded ash pots and scuttles of gleaming brass that catch the light in old paintings. From the Dutch East Indies they brought pewter for dinner plates, serving platters, and drinking mugs. The hinged lids of the latter gave rise to the Dutch proverb, "If you want the last drop from the mug, the lid will fall on your nose."

Each town had its distinctively styled pewter decanter, which was used by the town council for pouring wine for guests. The Amsterdam town jug had a modest belly between a slender foot and neck and a gracefully curved handle. To keep the cost down as a gift item, pewterers don't copy it true to size anymore. The modern version stands only twenty inches high and holds just over two cups of liquid. Such a jug would hardly seem appropriate for slaking the thirst of erstwhile town regents having one of their gargantuan meals! Another popular piece is the brandy cup, a low bowl having two flat, triangular-shaped handles with open leafwork. Formerly used for drinking brandy, the cups now serve nicely for holding paper clips, butter mints, and similar small items.

There is an abundant variety of contemporary pitchers and tea sets as well as copies of the town jugs and mugs of the past. Pewterware is still polished by hand to a dull antique or glossy finish.

Why pewterers are concentrated in Tiel on the Waal, no one knows. They passed on their skills from father to son, and apparently no one moved away from Tiel. It now calls itself "Pewter Town of The Netherlands," and takes pride in its pewter firms, one of which is "royal."

To honor the past, the Royal Metalware Factory Daalderop markets a series of twenty-eight old artisan figurines just under three inches tall, who carry water, blow glass, coop barrels, and of course, pour pewter.

Antique hunters can have fun in The Netherlands. Collectors of pewter treasure a buckled plate fished out of a river or a mug yielded by the hull of a sunken ship found when the Zuiderzee was drained. Old tiles, often with lumps of cement at the back where they were hacked out of demolished walls, are still fairly easy to find. Harder to find— and much, much harder on the pocketbook—are antique pendulum clocks that still keep accurate time after hundreds of years.

Fortunately, respectable copies of antique wall clocks are made, still partially by hand, so no one has to feel that he or she is buying a mass-produced model.

A *schippertje* ("little skipper") has an anchor in its pendulum and a carved wheel in its "tail," which is the wall panel that extends below the case holding the clockwork. A brass cylinder is attached to a pulley wheel, which goes down a double chain each time the clock strikes on the hour or the half. The weight has to be pulled up regularly, usually twice a day. If it is allowed to hang at the end of the chain, the clock stops.

An *Amsterdammertje* ("little Amsterdammer") is not so little. From the top of its arched canopy to the tip of its walnut tail, the clock averages thirty inches. A gilded atlas bent down under a globe and two trumpeting angels add more height to the top of the clock.

The case of a Frisian *stoeltjesklok* ("little chair clock") sits on four wooden knobs on a little platform. The clock has a very short tail depicting an hourglass centered between an angel wing and a bat wing to remind one and all that good and evil are with us as time goes on. Gilded, bugle-blowing mermaids hug the sides of the clock. Roses are strewn around the Roman numerals on the clock face, and above the face there may be painted a coach pulled by four white horses and carrying black-hatted men waving handkerchiefs.

The chain links are formed from a straight brass pin with a pair of pliers. According to Hinne Zweering, who had a Frisian clock shop in Amsterdam until he retired after fifty years as a clock maker, "A machine-made chain will never be as durable. It's the chain that's largely responsible for the accuracy of the timepiece." In an hour Mr. Zweering could pinch several yards of chain.

Shopping for Dutch handicrafts can be a delight in itself. In Arnhem's Open Air Museum, summertime visitors wander among windmills and replicas of early Dutch homes while they watch artisans at work. Pewterers work all year long in Rotterdam's House of the Sack Carriers Guild, once a meeting place for what was the Renaissance equivalent of a longshoremen's union. There you may watch them oversee their cauldron of bubbling metal, pour it into molds, and polish mugs, spoons, and brandy cups.

In Amsterdam the opening of the Holland Art and Craft Centre next door to the Sonesta Hotel is planned for the summer of 1980. Cigar makers, potters, silversmiths, and artists decorating wooden and pottery wares will show visitors how their handicrafts are made from start to finish. In addition, the center will present "The Amsterdam Experience," a multi-screen video and sound show on the city's history.

Artisans also ply their trades at summer country fairs, where visitors may acquire an unexpected bonus. Almost all of the national annual production of two million pairs of wooden shoes is machine made, for wear by part-time gardeners and full-time farmers, who may go through a pair every six weeks. And yet at country fairs, one may still find an occasional wood carver using simple tools to shape *klompen* from pieces of willow wood. What could be a more typically Dutch souvenir to bring home than a hand-carved *klompje*?

Hikers cross the tidal flats in Friesland.

CHAPTER 16

HIKING AND BIKING

A PARTY OF HIKERS led by a guide walks along a narrow, fragile-looking osier dam. Everyone balances precariously on the willow twigs that are matted into a barrier three feet high. Beyond lies the Wadden Sea, a seemingly endless expanse of water and haze. It is six o'clock in the morning, and the hikers' destination, an offshore sandbar, is still invisible. These hardy souls are taking part in a uniquely Dutch sport known as *wadlopen*, which takes its name from the *wadden*, the shallows of the Wadden Sea.

When the dam comes to an end, the hikers step into black alluvial mud. With an ominous sucking sound, it envelops their feet and legs up to the knees. The guide plants his pole, leans on it to take a step, and then pulls it from the muck in readiness for the next stride. The hikers follow suit, and soon their high-topped basketball shoes fill with mud. Some of them wear sneakers secured with elastic bandages as if they had ankle sprains. The reason becomes apparent when one man loses a shoe and decides to leave it behind. He regrets his decision as soon as his stockinged foot hits a sharp-edged shell.

The mud gives way to firm, clean sand, first covered with a few inches of water and then, as the tide further ebbs, exposed in wavy ripples. The hikers are walking now in a dream world of light and puddles of sparkling water. Mussels glow a deep purple in the sun, and a tern swoops down in search of food. All that can be seen of the Friesland coast is the church tower in Wierum.

When the *wadlopers* reach the sandbar, they are surrounded by hundreds of birds wheeling overhead and their fuzz-covered young, who sprint between tufts of marram grass. The guide allows only a fifteen-minute lunch break. On the way back they wade through gullies where the water runs waist-high. By the time they reach the shore, an hour and a half later, the sea has covered their tracks. The timing was right.

Once it wasn't. In the late 1960s I made the crossing with a Leeuwarden guide, two Dutch university students, and nine American girls I was piloting through Europe. After the guide told us we should go back, he realized that he had let us play too long. Our departure would have to be delayed until the next low tide, six hours hence.

Six hours of playing Robinson Crusoe on a glorious day seemed fun, but our organized tour group had a schedule to meet and reserved hotel rooms to reach. The Dutch boys— strong swimmers both—offered to go back and summon a boat. When they reached the shore, they walked right into the Dutch water-watching apparatus. A dike guard with binoculars had followed their progress from afar and alerted the national police. A sixty-eight-year-old retired fisherman from nearby Moddergat was ready with a sloop and outboard motor.

Mr. Visser putt-putted to the sandbar and brought us all back over water where we had walked on sand just a few hours before. On the dike the girls were interviewed by the press, and their comments appeared in the *Leeuwarder Courant* next to a photo of us stepping out of the sloop. The article included a firm reprimand to the guide. The trip had been made under normal conditions, and he should have watched the clock. What kind of Dutchman doesn't respect the water!

Wadlopen guides now carry walkie-talkies and keep in constant touch with the shore. On a nice day a hundred people may make the crossing although it is possible that the frequency of such trips will be restricted in the future for ecological reasons.

Organized walks of one kind or another are a national pastime. All over the land, on weekends or long summer evenings, walkers cover a prescribed number of miles and receive a piece of paper or a medal to prove they have performed the feat. Sports clubs and tourist associations eager to promote their area sponsor these walks.

Hikers by the hundreds plod for six days along the sandy North Sea beach from the Hook of Holland to Den Helder— a distance of eighty-five miles—and sleep in tents along the way. Others take the same amount of time to cover 120 miles and walk through the eleven towns of Friesland. They spend the night in "sleeping boats," which are thoroughly cleaned freight barges that have their holds filled with beds and mattresses. Ashore, the hikers wash in tents that are folded by the boat skippers each day and re-erected at the next overnight spot.

Here participation is limited to three hundred. "We can't cope with more, because there aren't enough places to eat in the smaller towns," wrote a member of the organizing committee. "We like to have dinner together; it enhances the trip's *gezelligheid* [the state of being cozy and intimate]."

The Frisian Eleven Town Hike has been organized annually since the years of World War II when the occupying Germans prohibited the International Four Days Distance March in Nijmegen, and the Dutch, not about to take no for an answer, walked in Friesland instead.

The Nijmegen march was resumed after the Germans left. The *vierdaagse*, as it is popularly called, was offered for the first time in 1909, and the walk has now been "done" by

three generations of Dutch families. It is held in July and
starts and ends each day in Nijmegen. Daily routes go
through different rural areas in loops of varying lengths
determined by age and sex, and control cards are stamped
along the way. Men between nineteen and forty-nine walk
thirty miles a day; men between fifty and sixty-four and
women between sixteen and fifty-five, twenty-four miles a
day; and men over sixty-five take the "light" eighteen-mile-
a-day course, joined by women over fifty-six and boys and
girls twelve to fifteen.

Accommodating the sixteen to seventeen thousand walkers who turn up each year takes a wholehearted community
effort. They are lodged in schools, private homes, and
military barracks. On one day of the march, a pontoon bridge
is laid over the Meuse near Cuyk over which the walkers
pass. Water traffic on that part of the river is stopped. Along
each day's route there are first aid stations with Red Cross
volunteers who treat blisters caused by inappropriate footwear and the endless pounding on hard-surfaced roads. On
rainy days the volunteers massage countless leg muscles
cramped from the effort of negotiating slick pavement.
Farmers put out milking buckets with water, and when it's
hot, they hose down anyone who asks for it. Flags fly from
the homes, and bands play in encouragement. A soft drink
company hands out free samples of orange pop while young
women from a perfume firm spray eau de cologne on the
walkers' necks and hands.

Only 5 percent of those who start the first day fail to finish
all four days. *Willen is Kunnen* ("if you want to, you can") is
painted in large letters above the check-out and check-in
booths in Nijmegen.

The walkers' triumphal entry into Nijmegen on the last
day is called the Gladiator March. It is a suitable name since
Roman heroes of long ago could not have enjoyed greater

admiration than these thousands of men and women who have walked for four days, sometimes in sultry heat or pouring rain. They march into town carrying flowers and singing the vierdaagse song, which ends,

> We are one for all,
> And all for one,
> So we'll go through Netherland,
> And through life as well.

Military units that have taken part in the march pass in review, their flags and regimental standards flying, by high-ranking officers and ambassadors from participating countries. Seated comfortably on everything from old sofas to overturned garbage cans, townspeople and proud friends and relatives cheer the marchers on. Reporters search their ranks for newsmakers, such as the seventy-two-year-old grandmother who has completed the march twenty-nine times. The exhilaration and camaraderie of these last few moments are a well-deserved reward.

For every Dutch person who enjoys the group walk, another wouldn't dream of it and joins friends or family on independent hikes over the footpaths marked *wandelpad* that lace the countryside.

Members of the Vereniging tot Behoud van Natuur-monumenten in Nederland ("Association for Preservation of Nature Monuments in The Netherlands") usually carry the club's handbook. It lists by province the nature monuments belonging to the association, as well as nature preserves, public forest lands, areas belonging to private conservation organizations, and the thousand or more private estates which are open to the public.

Some of these areas are no more than a clump of trees or a trail-lined marsh where migratory birds settle. The country's national park, De Hoge Veluwe, covers thirteen thousand acres of woods, sand dunes, and moors where the heather blooms a deep purple in August and September. Mating deer, however, cause part of the meandering park trails to be closed from the beginning of September to mid-October so that only motor traffic is allowed. Other areas are closed off in the spring to protect birds during their nesting season. The handbook alerts walkers to these contingencies.

Many Dutch make leisurely forays on bicycles. They pedal along quiet country roads and the six hundred miles of flat, well-laid-out bicycle paths that run next to highways, skirt waterways, and wander off over heathery moors. A path marked *fietspad* or *rijwielpad* is for bikers only. Those displaying a picture of a bicycle are also used by motorized bikes, which are avoided, whenever possible, by travelers relying on pedal power.

The fact that there are nine million bicycles for fourteen million people shows that they are a major means of transportation in The Netherlands. Dutch bicycles are utility vehicles having one or three speeds, fat tires, fenders, and mudguards. The rear wheels are equipped with skirt or coat protectors and luggage carriers from which plastic or canvas panniers hang. Don't be surprised if you see a family of five neatly distributed over two bicycles. Mother carries child no. 1 in a seat on her luggage carrier. Father accommodates child no. 2 in the same way, and child no. 3 perches on a seat in front of father.

Every so often the group spirit also gets to the bikers, and they set forth on organized distance rides to earn a certificate or medal upon completion. A four-day bicycle trip called the *fietsvierdaagse* is patterned after the Nijmegen vierdaagse. Bikers begin and end at the same place and ride a different route each day that is, however, of a length they choose. In 1979, seven group biking tours were organized, and the one in Drenthe drew seventeen thousand cyclists.

When I "did" the Bosbad Brabantia fietsvierdaagse in Hoeven, I joined a group of seven hundred and fifty. Some rode daily loops of one hundred kilometers (sixty miles). Most of these cyclists rode lightweight ten speeds and merely joined to get in training for bigger things. Others rode sixty or forty kilometers a day (thirty-six and twenty-four miles respectively). The latter distance was popular with parents who came with their children.

The emphasis was on getting to know North Brabant, and a list of museums and old churches was issued daily with the route instructions. Relaxation was another theme of the tour. To prevent riders from barreling along at top speed just to see how quickly they could cover their daily distance, volunteers manned the control posts in roadside cafes only at certain times. Speedy riders had to wait to get their card stamped or they wouldn't get the commemorative medal at the end of four days.

Because departure times were staggered—with the "hundreds" leaving first—and because bikers went off sightseeing, the country roads and bicycle paths were rarely crowded. At times no other bikers were in sight.

On the last day, after everyone had come in, the mayor of Hoeven made a speech and gave out prizes to the youngest participant (six), to the oldest (eighty-three), and to the one who had come from the farthest away (a distinction easily won by this biker, who came all the way from California).

Skating is a cherished winter sport in The Netherlands, but unfortunately the weather has not cooperated in recent years. For many winters the Dutch have been unable to skate from town to town over the canals—a picture familiar to anyone who has read *Hans Brinker or The Silver Skates.* The Eleven Town Skating Race in Friesland has not taken place since 1964. This grueling course of 120 miles takes some twelve hours of hard riding in a bitterly cold wind, over ice often ribbed like a washboard or full of gashes. For some riders the race has meant frostbite or fractured bones.

The Dutch, however, are not about to give up the idea of skating on their canals. My cousin Pien had this to say of the winter of 1978:

> Fortunately it is usually possible, even for one day, in January or February, to skate on natural ice. And then such a typical Dutch atmosphere prevails. Stalls sell hot chocolate and hot anise milk. Youngsters learning to skate push chairs ahead of them while jaunty grandparents skate arm in arm. Families stay together by skating one behind the other, each with an arm hooked over a long pole. Others with more skill speed along, joined together in a human chain, against the reddish winter sun.
>
> Early this year we went skating with a group of our friends near Giethoorn. It was beautiful—over lakes and little canals, through nature preserves and along the fields where rush was drying. It's cut after the frost when it can be easily reached over the ice. I find something like this better than skiing in Austria or Switzerland.

The following year brought a cold, cold winter that the Dutch will long remember. For weeks temperatures remained below freezing. There was ice aplenty, but also a lot of snow on top. And below the snow much of the ice was not strong enough for distance touring. "The children were disappointed," wrote Pien. "They had looked forward to trying the new skates they received at Sinterklaas."

Like many Dutch children, Eva and Martientje ride on Frisian *doorlopers* ("through-runners"). The blades have a curl in front and are set in wood like the skates in Avercamp's seventeenth-century ice paintings. They come with a leather heel that fits around the skater's shoe and with leather or webbed straps to tie the skate to the shoe. No one who has skated on "Frisians" as a child is likely to forget the misery of sitting on a canal bank, trying to undo the knots, while hands ungloved for the chore quickly chill.

The waters may withhold pleasures from the Dutch in winter by not freezing over, but they provide pleasures a hundredfold in other seasons. One-sixth of the country's surface is water, and the Dutch put every river, canal, creek, lake, estuary, and inland sea to good use in their leisure time.

They take to the water in a wide variety of pleasure craft. The vogue now is owning an old-fashioned wooden sailboat —the older the better—which is pampered and polished with the same love antique car buffs shower on their vintage automobiles. Other popular craft include the fifteen-foot B.M. (Bergumermeer) and the traditional forty-to-fifty-foot flat bottoms that fishermen used in shallow waters. These boats provide plenty of room for sleeping, and touring by boat—sailboat or motorboat—is a favorite way of spending a weekend or a vacation. Travelers under sail are often lucky enough to flag down a "shop on wheels" on its way to outlying farms. Towns and villages on the water are close together. All have places to moor, and terraces where sailors may sit and swap tales. The Dutch waterways, however, provide their own kind of challenges.

The big rivers and canals are crowded with tankers and big barges. In the still, silent air of a bird sanctuary where outboard motors are banned, a skipper may have to pull his boat along a towpath. On the Wadden Sea he has to know how to calculate tide and currents lest he be left high and dry on a sandbank as the tide ebbs. And locks are yet another matter. They are everywhere because the country's water housekeeping requires changing the water levels in canals and rivers to keep the low land from flooding. In the summer

you may join a long line of boats waiting their turn to go
through a lock. Since the lock keeper allows just so many to
enter the chamber at a time, you will have to endure the
following procedure if you're the first one in the next group:

- The lock keeper closes the gates of the chamber on the
  near side lets the water out of the chamber until it
  reaches the level of the water on the far side, and opens
  the far gates.
- Everyone in the chamber unties his boat and leaves at
  his own pace.
- A group of boats going in the opposite direction enters
  the chamber and ties up.
- The lock keeper closes the far gates, pumps the water in,
  opens the gates on the near side again, and lets the
  opposite traffic out.
- It's your turn to enter the lock, and now the children
  have wandered off in a meadow to pick flowers or
  pursue a butterfly.

Water traffic has the right of way over road traffic. In
principle this means that any skipper whose mast is too tall to
go under a bridge can blow his horn and expect the bridge to
be pulled upward or turned sideways to let his boat through,
while motorists wait patiently in a long line. But on main
roads the bridges have set opening hours. And on Sundays
some bridges—and locks for that matter—don't open at all or
work on a restricted schedule. A boater's almanac issued by
the Royal Dutch Touring Club tells you everything about
opening and closing times of locks and bridges. No fees are
levied, but it is customary to put a silver coin in the small
wooden shoe the bridge tender swings from a string on a pole
towards the passing boater.

Next to the boater's almanac, every vessel should have on board the boating regulations in Dutch water—a guide to a complicated game of priorities.

The Dutch waters, however, also provide enormous pleasure to people without a boat: the country's fishermen. Fishing is often considered the no. 1 national sport.

By the thousands, anglers flock to rivers and canals, bringing their folding chairs, big black fishing umbrellas, and poles, most of which are the new kind that telescope to a length of seven meters (twenty feet), and then they sit by the hour. The water is so muddy that anglers cannot tell whether a perch or a pike has swallowed their bait until they haul the fish out on shore.

Clubs of angling enthusiasts meet regularly early in the morning and enter contests. A hundred fishermen may be spread out, for example, along the carefully stocked moat of Naarden fortress. A prize is awarded to the person who catches the greatest length of fish laid together heads to tails. The fish are kept alive in a "living net" in the water until they are measured by a club inspector and then usually put back.

For every hiker, boater, and angler enjoying the Dutch countryside, a car is probably parked somewhere. The fact that so many outdoorbound must *drive* to their fresh air and exercise is a big problem in The Netherlands. At the end of a weekend, cars on access roads to urban centers cause gigantic traffic jams. Then many Dutch say to each other, "Next weekend, let's stay quietly in town." But the next weekend the sun is shining, or it looks as if it will be shining, and the Dutch take to their cars again. Like the tides that pulse back and forth against the sea dikes, the traffic moves in and out of the cities on every holiday and weekend—a seemingly uncontrollable force.

Men and women from Wijdenes dance in their former regional dress at a weekly "historical" market in Hoorn, North Holland.

CHAPTER 17

WOODEN SHOES AND WINDMILLS

LONG SKIRTS WHIRL and tails of frock coats fly as the couples
in the photograph opposite swing to a cheery accordionist's
beat. They are performing a dance called "The Mill" and
wear traditional West Frisian dress.

The bonnets of handmade lace are made with little pleats
in the back that stick out like a duck's tail, and they are
anchored to the head with golden "ear irons." The silver-
clasped bags are made of tiny beads. Bonnets and bags are
heirlooms, but the women's dresses and the men's black suits
are copies of clothes that not so long ago were worn on
Sundays and festive occasions. The people donned a simpler
version for everyday wear.

In West Friesland (so called because it belonged to
Friesland in the Middle Ages), five additional dance groups
made up of dedicated amateurs appear at other "historical"
markets, evening entertainments, and convalescent homes
and other places where people need cheering up. Dance
groups in Friesland and other provinces do the same. Each
group dons the dress which was once indigenous to its region
or village but, like the West Frisian dress, is worn no more.

In the past, the number of local costumes in daily use was
enormous. In 1805 a writer described The Netherlands as
"A small piece of the earth with larger variety in dress than
nearly all continents outside Europe combined. The various
northern areas of the realm seem inhabited by extraordinary

people. The fishing and farming villages,the islands and the coasts all have their own characteristic dress."

Now the dress is alive in only a dozen places, and it is worn mostly by older women. The fabrics needed for the finery are expensive, and the styling is eminently unsuitable for the fast-paced, mobile lifestyle of Dutch young people. They find it impractical for sitting on the motorized bicycles called *brommers* (mopeds) and far too time consuming to put on.

In her delightful and beautifully photographed book, *Klederdrachten*, Constance Nieuwhoff includes a series of photos of a Marken woman dressing. The island of Marken was not linked to the mainland until the Zuiderzee was dammed off, a fact that may explain why the dress has changed little in four hundred years. The women of Marken may have been too isolated to learn of new dress trends or just too poor to follow them. At any rate, the style of the traditional dress resembles that worn by a well-to-do towns-woman of the sixteenth century: a bonnet, linen shirt with puffed sleeves, skirt, apron, shawl, and *kraplap* (a collar covering the shoulders and chest for the purpose of prevent-ing the chills easily incurred by the then-fashionable plunging necklines).

Here's what a woman from Marken has to do after she gets up. She slips into a striped petticoat and pulls on a long-sleeved blouse. Over the blouse she layers a brightly colored embroidered bodice laced in front, a red woolen bib pinned to the bodice, a bolero, and a frontal piece of flowered chintz pinned to the bolero. This piece replaces the early kraplap. Then she puts on a black skirt and an apron. On an upturned jug she now builds her little pillbox bonnet by folding together seven pieces of cloth, a confection of white cotton, red wool, handmade lace, and flowered chintz. The bonnet is worn jauntily on the back of her head like a nurse's cap. The larger bonnet of years past consisted of twelve pieces and was built by a friend or family member right on the woman's head. She slept with the bonnet on, half-sitting in her bedstead built in the wall.

A Marken man rarely wears the traditional dress anymore, but if he does, it's the sporty little cap and black, baggy pants adapted to the fishing trade that most Marken men formerly followed. The material is homespun wool, windproof and water-repellent, and the loose-fitting garment reaches halfway down the calves.

The baggy pants of nearby Volendam men, if they wear the dress, reach down to the feet. "Longpants," the men of Marken call the Volendammers. The women of Volendam wear striped skirts and black aprons, triple-layered, thick-beaded coral chokers with gold clasps in front, and lace caps with curling edges that look like opened-up tulips upside down. This is the dress frequently shown on Dutch tourist brochures.

Marken and Volendam, towns which are only a short drive north of Amsterdam, have resigned themselves to being tourist attractions. Annually, hundreds of tour buses spill their passengers from many nations over the two villages. In other regional dress holdouts, tourists with cameras tend to be less welcome. But how tempting it is to photograph! The dress varies according to the area and the occasion. There are different costume touches for summer and winter, everyday and holiday, and for light and deep mourning. When a woman is not in mourning, the people of Marken say that she is "in the wild colors."

In Spakenburg, a fishing village on Lake IJssel, a woman wears a heavily starched, figure-concealing kraplap that arches like a bridge over her shoulders to her waist. It is white cotton with brilliantly colored flowers if she is "in the wild colors," and dark purple or black cotton with flowers in muted tones if she is mourning. When fishing was the exclusive means of livelihood in a village, many women were in mourning for men lost at sea.

On her head the Spakenburg woman wears a little black cap covered by a hand-crocheted bonnet in her own pattern.

In the seaside resort of Scheveningen, women wear white, boat-shaped bonnets that hang low on their necks. Their "ear irons" are two gold ornaments that extend from gold wire on the front of their bonnets near the crown. All year long the women wear long black woolen skirts, topped in winter by pelerines and in summer by fringed shawls in pastel colors. The square shawl is folded diagonally and pleated in the back with safety pins to make room for the drooping back of a full bonnet.

White caps as big as sails are worn by women in Zeeland. Visitors have the feeling that if one rode her bicycle with the wind at her back, she wouldn't have to pedal at all. She could sail along on her wings.

Abroad it is commonly believed that the Dutch wear wooden shoes with their traditional clothes. For dress-up they usually wear low-heeled black leather shoes, which sometimes have ornate silver buckles over the instep. Wooden shoes are for scrubbing stoops, hoeing in the garden, or digging up potatoes in the fields.

For centuries the Dutch have recognized how practical wooden shoes are. They don't deteriorate as quickly in mud and water as leather shoes do, and when filled with straw, they keep the feet warm. They are easy to clean and easy to slip into or out of when a person is leaving or entering the house. And wooden shoes are inexpensive compared with leather shoes and rubber boots.

Such footwear is now replacing some of the wooden shoes, but each year two million pairs are manufactured. The image of "Holland, land of windmills and wooden shoes," still holds true.

As for windmills, nine hundred fifty of them are preserved as national monuments, pampered by the National Service for Monument Care, local authorities, and private organizations such as the Dutch Windmill Association. About a third of the mills are still operated by professional millers or members of the Volunteer Millers Guild who are certified as millers after taking a course of instruction given by the Dutch Windmill Association. The certificate is a must for anyone who wants to operate one of the national monuments. Like the professional millers, the amateurs live in the windmill, but work it only during their leisure time.

Windmills have different functions, and thus they come in different shapes and sizes.

Industrial mills, which grind grain or saw wood, are frequently in towns where they have to be tall so that the arms can catch the wind above the buildings. Often cylindrical and made of stone, they may reach a height of seven stories.

The *tjaskers* of Friesland are the smallest ones. Once started, they work without human supervision. Looking somewhat like a praying mantis, the wooden tjasker inclines on a meadow by the side of a canal. Its arms connect without cogwheels or other transmission mechanism to a shaft that slopes to the ground and pumps water with an Archimedes screw. Ten years ago, only a few idle tjaskers were left. Now a dozen new ones have been built, and most of them pump water in nature preserves.

In the provinces of North and South Holland, stout polder mills, their sides thatched with reed, rise majestically at the water's edge. With nothing taller than a cow to compete with, they dominate the flat landscape. Three operate in the Aarlanderveenpolder near Alphen-aan-de-Rijn under the jurisdiction of a tiny "watership," a semiautonomous water authority that likes to keep the polder dry with these three mills as if the electric pump had not been invented.

The sixteen polder mills clustered around Kinderdijk near Rotterdam work every Saturday afternoon during July and August. Under favorable wind conditions, they perform for the benefit of tourists. Tour buses spill thousands here, and many a photographer has felt his head swim while trying to focus on the lofty windmill arms, all turning at different angles.

One of the Kinderdijk mills is open to the public on these "open house" days. There are other windmills in The Netherlands that can be visited while they are in operation, and it's an opportunity no one should miss. The arms turn a shaft inside that inclines slightly from front to rear, high in the mill's attic called the "cap." Via a transmission mechanism, the shaft rotates a king post that passes through the center of several floors and makes great oak cogwheels mesh into each other. These wheels transmit motion to the Archimedes screw that pumps water, or to the saw or millstones. The millstones of a flour mill consist of the stationary bedstone at the bottom and the runner stone that revolves above it; the contact sides of the stones are provided with spiral furrows for grinding. Millstones may be five feet in diameter and twelve inches thick.

Windmills speak a language all their own. When their arms form a cross ($+$), they are ready to work. When the windmill wants to rest, its arms make an X. Arms rotated counterclockwise so that one of the arms is just after twelve noon indicate a happy celebration such as a birth or a wedding. When the arms are set just before noon, they speak of mourning. During World War II, the language of the windmills was used to relay messages to resistance workers. When the news came that the war was over, the arms of all the country's windmills cried, "Hoorah!"

Many windmills have names, showing the popular affection in which they were held. "Housewife," "The People's

Friend," and "The Shepherd" are three of them. The names, which usually date back to the time of the mills' construction, maybe hundreds of years ago, are sculpted in wood on the gaily painted "beard" just under the cap.

In the past, windmills were very much part of Dutch life. They performed an important role in creating new land and keeping people's feet dry by pumping water as well as grinding flour, sawing wood, pressing oil from hempseed, and churning rags into paper pulp. They were often a social center, as townspeople waited their turn with a sack of grain or a chopped-down tree. A century ago, nine thousand windmills worked hard. Old loyalties are renewed today when a windmill is restored, often from shambles, and the completion of the restoration is a happy event. The mill is decorated with flags flying between its arms, and the local people dance below. The mill takes up where it left off when it was idled by the arrival of the steam engine, and later, electricity. It may provide a livelihood once more for a miller, or merely turn from time to time to show how it works. This keeps the mill in good shape. Like cars, windmills should be used.

Alas, occasionally a windmill burns down. Lightning strikes it or heat builds up under the cap and sets the windmill ablaze. Or a windmill has to make way for urban expansion or an industrial plant. In such a case, however, the windmill may be moved somewhere else—to the Open Air Museum in Arnhem, perhaps, or a public park. In 1961, a mill dating from 1636 was moved to the southwest corner of Amsterdam near the Amstel river, where it now handles the underground drainage for the suburb of Buitenveldert. The mill's mighty, wind-powered arms turn against a backdrop of tall concrete apartment buildings with TV antennas atop.

Country roads are often made of red brick baked from river clay. When a road begins to sag, workers remove bricks, fill up the low spot with sand, and replace the bricks.

CHAPTER 18

TIPS FOR TRAVELERS

IF YOU'RE PLANNING to visit The Netherlands on your own, there are several organizations to assist you in choosing what to see and how to find it.

Before leaving home, contact one of The Netherlands National Tourist Offices. (See address list in Appendix B.) In The Netherlands, stop by one of the four hundred local or provincial tourist associations with the melodious initials VVV (Vereniging voor Vreemdelingenverkeer). The VVVs provide lists of attractions to suit any fancy, and their services are free. The smallest towns have a VVV, and the hostesses all speak English. They have built up a reputation for being helpful and will even make phone calls to find you a room if you appear in person rather than telephone. Look for their standard sign: an upside-down triangle with three Vs inside.

The best road maps are those of the Royal Dutch Touring Club (ANWB). Thirteen sectional maps show castles, windmills, pumping stations, churches worth visiting, nature preserves, and scenic routes. On the map, black symbols accompanied by four-digit numbers correspond to numbers on ANWB directional road signs. Red symbols with five-digit numbers correspond to numbers on the low markers the Dutch call *paddestoelen* ("mushrooms") because of their distinctive shape.

You can buy the maps from any of the forty-odd ANWB

offices in The Netherlands if you are a member of the
ANWB or an affiliated foreign automobile club like the
AAA. (Be sure to have your membership card with you.)
Otherwise, you can buy local ANWB maps at a bookstore
or VVV.

There is so much to see and do in The Netherlands that
you may not only indulge your favorite interests, but also de-
velop new ones along the way.

Are castles your thing? The Netherlands has small,
intimate ones that won't wear you out. A little gem close to
Amsterdam is Muiden Castle. Built in the thirteenth century
by an unfortunate count who was later murdered there, it has
a moat and drawbridge and watchtowers at the corners of
thick, thick walls. Suits of armor worn by the early occupants
are on display in one of the timbered rooms. Their construction makes the visitor wonder how those brave knights sat
down.

For a homier touch, visit Menkemaborg, twenty miles
north of Groningen in Uithuizen. Although it was built as a
fortified stronghold with a wide moat, it is more typical of an
eighteenth-century manor house. A lovely rose garden,
period furnishings, and exquisite porcelains give visitors a
glimpse of its gracious past.

Casinos? Yes, The Netherlands has them, just like Las
Vegas or Monte Carlo. The Calvinist burghers of yesteryear
wouldn't have believed it, and some of today's burghers can't
quite believe it, either. In Zandvoort on the North Sea, in
Scheveningen a little farther down the coast, and in Valken-
burg, Limburg, you can play roulette and blackjack.

Churches? In the provinces of Groningen and Friesland
are brick Romanesque churches on the mounds the early
settlers built to stay above water. Their peaked "saddle
roofs" on sturdy square towers were purportedly made so
that witches would have a place to rest outside the church.

The mound church of Hichtum, Friesland, is tiny. When you have found the farmer across the road who has the key and stand inside, you feel you could stretch your arms from one whitewashed wall to the other.

The country's largest church is probably the Church of Saint John in Gouda. It has sixty-four huge stained-glass windows, which taken together would cover half an acre in shimmering, jewel-like tones. One of them depicts William of Orange, the "George Washington" of The Netherlands. (Before you visit, find out when the church is open to visitors.)

You'll find Saint John's Cathedral in 's Hertogenbosch, North Brabant. Built between the early 1300s and 1530, the monumental Gothic edifice ranks with the French cathedrals. Sculpted stone figures look down from flying buttresses. Somewhere off the long and stately nave you'll find a marvelously intricate brass baptismal font crafted in 1492. The font cover is adorned with a tiered "Gothic tower" with arches, and spires, and statues. The ornamentation reaches so high that you have to crane your neck to see the top.

Maastricht has the Cathedral of Saint Servatius, consecrated in the eleventh century to honor the town's first bishop, who died in 384. On display in the treasury are a gilded, gem-studded shrine in the shape of a house, which contains partial remains of the saint, and Saint Peter's Key, a twelve-inch key once believed to encase in its hollow handle a tiny piece of the chain that shackled Saint Peter to the wall of his Roman prison. Every seven years a pilgrimage is held, during which these and other holy relics are carried in procession through the streets of Maastricht. In 1976 twelve men carried a platform with the shrine under a canopy fringed with gold. Boys in acolyte robes carried busts of saints, followed by groups of girls with solemn faces. Each group, dressed alike in flowing robes, moved in unison with

slow, dancelike steps. Two thousand people walked in the
procession that year. In the evening, on the tree-lined
square, the history of the relics was told in a spectacular
sound and light show.

Museums? The Netherlands may well have more per
capita than any other country in the world. A few years ago,
KLM Royal Dutch Airlines published a guide to more than
four hundred.

Among the internationally famous Dutch art museums,
the National Gallery in Amsterdam is the most visited.
Many people limit their tour of this museum to the *Night
Watch* and other Golden Age masterpieces, but other
collections also deserve time and attention. In the department of sculpture and applied arts you'll find—among
stunning tapestries, sculptures, silver, and furniture from the
Middle Ages to the twentieth century—an extraordinary
Delft blue tulip vase fashioned in 1700. It looks like a
Chinese pagoda, tapering upward with eleven square "stories,"
the corners of which are equipped with orifices for tulips.
Dollhouses, open in front and mounted on legs, show in
miniature every bit of furniture, furnishing, and utensil in
every room in an eighteenth-century patrician home, and
members of the household as well. A rich merchant would
order such a doll house as a decoration for his salon; the
children were not allowed to touch the expensive replicas. In
the Dutch history room are altar panels showing the 1421
Saint Elizabeth's flood. Ask the museum guard to show you
the cradle which a legendary cat kept afloat during the flood
and so saved the child inside. You can also stand in wonder
before the little bookcase in which Hugo de Groot escaped
from his prison in Loevestein Castle.

Just a few blocks away from the National Gallery are the
Van Gogh Museum and the Stedelijk ("municipal") Museum.
Sculptures by twentieth-century artists greet you from the

Stedelijk's front lawn, and inside is the latest in Dutch art in permanent collections and rotating exhibitions.

In The Hague's municipal museum—called the Gemeente Museum—the largest collection of Mondrians anywhere traces the artist's development from early landscapes to abstract art. The building is of interest to architecture buffs. It was designed by Hendrik Berlaghe, who in the early part of this century made a name for The Netherlands by building in a rational, functional way. To be considered beautiful in those days, a building had to have at least one Greek column, or a bit of baroque plaster, or a neogothic curve. The Gemeente Museum has straight, uncomplicated lines.

When in The Hague, you should not miss the Mauritshuis, which has another fine collection of Golden Age masters that is not quite so overwhelming as the one in the National Gallery. You may see a medical student from a faraway land stand in front of Rembrandt's *Anatomy Lesson* and marvel at the real thing. Prints of this canvas are hanging in medical schools around the world. Don't fail to look up at the ceilings in the exposition rooms. Many are of finely carved wood. The museum once was the residence of a prince of Orange named Maurits.

Special interest museums abound for everyone from children to scholars. Utrecht has a museum where you can view and hear music boxes and barrel organs, while vintage cars are exhibited at the Autroton in Drunen, North Brabant. In the same province is the city of Eindhoven, where Philips celebrated its seventy-fifth anniversary in 1966 by erecting the Evoluon. The building looks like a giant flying saucer and houses a sophisticated tribute to science and technology.

The Rijksmuseum van Oudheden ("National Museum of Antiquities") in Leiden offers something special to those with their eye on the distant past. Its collection of Egyptian, Greek, and Roman antiquities is small but of high quality.

The Dutch point with pride to a second-century statue of Nehallennia, a goddess to whom the Romans prayed before sailing to Great Britain from what is now Zeeland. In 1970 she was pulled from the Eastern Scheldt and relieved of the barnacles and silt that had accumulated over seventeen hundred years. Sitting straight up in her stone chair with her hands crossed in her lap, she reminds one of *Whistler's Mother.*

The Provincial Museum in Assen, Drenthe, offers more antiquities of native origin, including what may be the oldest canoe in the world. The Boat of Pesse, as it is called, has been dated by the radioactive carbon method at 6800 B.C. It was made from a Scotch pine log hollowed out by fire, and the story goes that the pine still oozes resin.

Also on display are earthenware storage pots in the shape of a funnel. These belonged to the Funnel Cup People who lived in Drenthe around 2500 B.C. They built group funeral chambers aboveground with enormous stones which archeologists think were carried from Norway by glaciers and left behind in Drenthe when the ice cap melted. One of these tombs, which the Dutch call *hunebedden*, has been resurrected in the museum. Some fifty others, carefully renovated, are scattered around Drenthe. The hunebedden used to be covered with sod, but now only the boulders are left. Some of these granite megaliths weigh half a ton and make one wonder how the early settlers moved them.

In June 1979 a new museum, the Rijksmuseum Catharijneconvent, opened in Utrecht. It was described in the newspaper as "unique in Europe." The article went on to say, "The church had an enormous hold on the life of our forefathers. A western society without church, dominie, or priest was unthinkable." The museum portrays chronologically—with paintings, sculptures, church robes, books, vessels, and architecture—how the Lowlands were christianized by Frankish and Irish monks. The exhibit concludes with a review of the relationship between Catholics and Protestants of the nineteenth and twentieth centuries and the current status of religion in The Netherlands.

Special attractions for children include the miniature town of Madurom in The Hague, where many of the country's famous buildings are shown at 1/25 scale. In North Brabant, seven miles north of Tilburg, is De Efteling, a recreation park which was the 1972 winner of La Pomme d'Or, a travel writers' award for the most attractive tourist attraction in Europe. Designed by the Dutch artist Anton Pieck, it is 375 acres of enchantment, where a life-size fakir flies back and forth on a carpet and Sleeping Beauty lies in the forest.

Music is big in The Netherlands. For its size, the country has a phenomenal number of chamber orchestras and at least a dozen symphony orchestras—all sustained in part by government subsidies. There is no lack of orchestral concerts from classical to avant-garde.

If you go to hear the Amsterdam Concertgebouw Orchestra at the Concertgebouw ("Concert Building") in Amsterdam, you may find yourself sitting in a section behind the orchestra, where those in the front row of the audience rub elbows with the harpist and bassoonist in the last row of the orchestra. You can see the conductor's facial expressions as he directs, and for a few delightful hours, you have the feeling that you are part of an orchestra that ranks among the world's finest.

Amateur choirs give performances all over the country. Among the best-known groups, with several records to its name, is the all-male Mastreechter Staar. This choir sings madrigals, Negro spirituals, folk ditties, and the *Saint Matthew's Passion*. Every Sunday morning and Thursday evening you can attend their rehearsals in Maastricht. Crescendo, the all-male Christian fishermen's choir from Urk, sings in traditional Urker black baggy pants and black jackets over gaily striped red shirts. They made a record entitled *Nederland en Oranje* after a song of the same name. Mixed church choirs give concerts in many a venerable House of God.

Organists give recitals on famous pipe organs in churches. Saint Michael's in Zwolle, Overijssel, has a 1721 Arp Schnitger, the Saint Bavo in Haarlem a 1738 Christiaan Müller, and there are many more. If you go to one of the organ concerts, dress warmly even in summer. The naves of these old churches never seem to lose their chill.

The Dutch also have a fair amount of live theater and *kleinkunst*, a form of cabaret art that is a Dutch speciality. While someone plays the piano or the guitar, a second person sings and often mocks recent events or politicians. Wim Kan and Corry Vonk, a husband-wife team, have been amusing full houses with their satirical wit for forty years. For foreign travelers, the theater, particularly the cabaret art with its references to the contemporary Dutch scene, is often hard to follow even with a knowledge of Dutch. The choirs and the concerts, the Dutch National Ballet, and The Netherlands Opera Foundation are all more likely to guarantee a successful evening of Dutch culture.

The Dutch tourist industry is always coming up with new ideas to lure travelers with dollars, yen, or marks to The Netherlands and to induce Dutch vacationers to spend their guilders at home. A few years ago, the provincial VVVs in Overijssel and Gelderland introduced individual "packaged" bicycle tours of two to nine days. Participants prepay meals and overnight accommodations and, with route description in hand, bike at their own pace from one overnight stop to the next. A rental bike with side panniers is provided. Most of the tours are routed along uncluttered country roads, and lodging is provided by quiet country hotels, the kind where you have to whisper in the dining room.

The most ambitious of the bicycle tours is the Holland Cross-Country Tour, a nine-day, 250-mile trip, which my daughter Madelyn and I made in 1979. After we had bicycled for close to two hours over the new 17-mile dike built right through Lake IJssel from Enkhuizen to Lelystad, we agreed that there is no better way to gain a sense of what all that Dutch water-draining business is about. The dike was just wide enough for a two-lane road and a bicycle path. On either side were choppy waves, and land was only dimly visible on the horizon. We spent the night in Lelystad, named after Ir. Lely, mastermind of the Zuiderzee works, and bicycled the next day over Eastern Flevoland with the neat bandbox look of a new polder.

If you prefer not to be tied down to a program, you may, of course, plot your own bicycle trip. Sturdy Dutch bicycles can be rented at numerous railway stations and bicycle shops. The Dutch are starting to ride ten speeds now, but these racing bikes are almost impossible to rent. Actually, you may be happier with a heavier weight vehicle when you ride on bicycle paths paved with square concrete tiles pushed up by the ever-shifting Dutch soil or on bumpy, secondary roads.

If you tour The Netherlands by car, there are a few conventions and conveniences you need to know. The distances, of course, are given in kilometers (1 kilometer equals 0.6 mile). Traffic from the right has priority. On the ring dikes that encircle the new polders, big road signs warn drivers to "turn on your lights" (*ontsteekt uw lichten*). People drive with lights on in broad daylight to avoid "polder blindness," a cause of serious accidents. With shimmering Lake IJssel on one side and flat land on the other, it is hard for drivers to see if other cars are traveling in the same direction or coming toward them.

Road signs are the international ones in use all over

Europe, but only in The Netherlands are there many red-bordered triangular signs showing a car falling off a wall, which means that a quai or river bank is ahead, and signs showing a drawbridge.

Yellow ANWB "talking poles" assist stranded motorists on major highways. They can just push the button on the pole and ask for help. A mechanic in a yellow ANWB car marked Wegenwacht comes to fix the car, and if he doesn't have the parts, he orders a tow truck. The service is free to ANWB members, but others pay on the spot.

If you're planning on doing much driving, you may want to avoid July and August, the vacation season when the Dutch are in motion and the inhabitants of neighboring nations flock to Dutch beaches on the North Sea. An especially busy time is *bouwvakvacantie*, the three-week vacation that Dutch construction workers take simultaneously, usually in July.

Public transportation is unparalleled for economy and often for convenience. Frequently scheduled trains criss-cross the country on time. Each station has white and blue pictograms to guide travelers to the information counter (a large *I*) and the ticket windows (two tickets with 2 and 1 superimposed). Dutch trains, like all European trains, have first and second class accommodations. First class costs about one and a half times as much as second class and almost always has seats available even in peak hours. Since the longest train ride by Intercity takes about four hours, one can go almost anywhere for lunch in a day. On most routes travelers are permitted to take their bicycles with them if they buy a ticket for the bike and load and unload it in the baggage car themselves. A personal pass with picture identification allows unlimited train travel for eight days without buying tickets.

While there are numerous city buses and streetcars in the

towns, you may find that the easiest way to get from one place to another is to walk. Few cities are so enormous that with the help of comfortable shoes, one can't cover at least the center on foot, and systems of boarding streetcars and buying tickets can be confusing to a newcomer. Sometimes one boards in front and buys a ticket from the driver; at other times one boards in back and buys a ticket from an automat or a conductor. Passengers who have bought a ticket booklet at a tobacco shop have to use the ticket-validating machine, usually located in the rear of the car. Failure to have a valid ticket is punishable with a fine. Ask the local VVV for help in mastering the transit system if you are in doubt about routes and methods of paying fares.

The Dutch have a reputation for being reserved, but as you walk around town in the evening, you won't think so. The drapes are open in many lighted living rooms so that a passerby may see precisely who is doing what. At this time of day all shops are closed except on Thursday, a "buying evening," when stores are open until nine o'clock. Be aware that the trades have different afternoons off during the week, but butchers or bakers in one town may take Tuesdays and Wednesdays off respectively, and in another town do the reverse. By law a store may not be open more than fifty-two hours a week. The hours have to be posted in a window. All stores are closed on Sundays, except an occasional *apotheek* ("pharmacy"), which specializes in medications. Toiletries are sold in a *drogisterij* ("drugstore"). A great variety of other specialty shops limit their merchandise to one type such as gloves, notions, lingerie, poultry and eggs, or produce.

Prices currently include a whopping 18-percent B.T.W. (added value tax), which may go up. Since personal checks are rarely accepted, carry traveler's checks or cash for your purchases.

Should you have to use a public telephone, try to find a

post office, marked P.T.T. for *"post, telefoon, telegraaf."*
The main post office in a city or town is usually open in the
evening. You go to the proper counter, fill out a slip, and are
assigned a telephone booth. You may talk as long as you wish
and pay at the counter when you are through. Wait for the
dial tone when you are dialing a Dutch area code. If the
information line is busy, you will hear a recorded voice
telling you how many people are waiting ahead of you. If it's
nine, for example, you hear, *"Het aantal wachtenden voor u
is negen"* ("The number of people waiting ahead of you is
nine") and you are informed of lower numbers until it's
your turn.

In case you have to spell a name for an operator, it helps to
know which names the Dutch use for the letters of the
alphabet. That way you can spell out a telegram address, for
example, or understand the operator when she fires at you,
"Nico, Utrecht, Ypsilon, Simon," after she has found the
name Nuys in the directory.

A-Anna	J-Jan	S-Simon
B-Bernard	K-Karel	T-Teunis
C-Cornelis	L-Lodewijk	U-Utrecht
D-Dirk	M-Marie	V-Victor
E-Eduard	N-Nico	W-Willem
F-Ferdinand	O-Otto	X-Xantippe
G-Gerard	P-Pieter	Y-Ypsilon
H-Hendrik	Q-Quadraat	IJ-IJmuiden
I-Izaäk	R-Rudolf	Z-Zaandam

If you are returning to The Netherlands after an absence of
some years, you may be surprised at the greater liberalism.
An American teenager on a recent visit commented on some
of the "funny" TV commercials. "There's one for peanuts
where a lady in a low-cut dress drops some down her front,

and a man decides to be nice and help her get them out. Or this guy holds up a bar because he wants a beer, and this lady in a strapless dress holds up her hands, and—"

In big light boxes on Amsterdam hotels, the silhouette of a naked woman flashes, advertising an escort guide service and a telephone number. Yes, it's what you think. The "service" is very classy and discreet, following a good dinner, dancing, and educated conversation. (Most of the escorts have college degrees.)

The class structure, so rigidly observed for centuries, is becoming less divisive. Intermarriages between persons from different classes don't cause the family upheavals they used to, just as intermarriages between the faiths have ceased to tear families apart.

The complaint has been heard that the Dutch are not so polite and friendly as they used to be. True, when you ask for directions in a busy department store, an occasional sales-person may ask, "Can't you see the sign?", but in a small shop the clerk still accompanies you to the door—an old Dutch custom.

Speaking Dutch is no prerequisite for receiving courteous treatment. Many Dutch learned at least some English in school and are glad to practice it on you. If they do not speak English, they make do with sign language and a smile.

The Dutch spirit of helpfulness seems to increase the farther one travels from the crowded Rim City. A few years ago, I parked a car in a driving rain on the Holwerd pier to take a ferry to Ameland, one of the Wadden Islands. When I returned the next day, I found a note on my dashboard: "Dear Sir, if you leave your car, you should lock it and turn off your lights. Now I've done it for you." It was signed, "Mevr. Jansen."

Peter Stuyvesant, the last Dutch governor of New Amsterdam. The people of Wolvega, Friesland, where he was born in 1592, call the statue Piet Poot ("Peter Wooden Leg").

CHAPTER 19

THE DUTCH IN THE U.S.A.

IN 1609 HENRY HUDSON, in command of a Dutch three-masted ship, reached the northeast coast of the New World and, trying to find a route to the Pacific, discovered the river now bearing his name. After he let it be known in The Netherlands that the Indians had beaver skins, Dutch traders made the long ocean voyage and founded small posts in the Hudson River valley to barter beads and mirrors with the Indians for the valuable pelts.

The Dutch discovery of the Hudson River and the Dutch presence in the valley gave the Republic of the Seven United Netherlands reason to claim a huge area located between the Delaware and Connecticut rivers. The Dutch West India Trading Company, which was already conducting a brisk trade in West Africa, Brazil, and the West Indies, received the exclusive trading right to the area, now called New Netherland. Local traders had to sell all exportable wares to the company.

At the entrance to the Hudson River, on the tip of Manhattan Island, the Dutch built a fort in 1626. According to one source, they paid the Delaware Indians "sixty guilders, ten shirts, eighty pairs of hose, ten guns, thirty bullets, thirty pounds of powder, thirty kettles and one copper frying pan" for the twenty-three thousand acres of land that was Manhattan Island. Goats and sheep grazed on the clay walls of the fortification, which were covered with sod as if they were dikes. A few mean-looking cannons were mounted on top.

The town of New Amsterdam grew haphazardly around the fort. Citizens staked their fences far into neighbors' fields and were indifferent to the fact that pigpens and outhouses jutted out into public roads. No one ever asked the governor, who represented the Dutch West India Trading Company, for permission to build, as company ordinances required. Even for a chicken coop His Excellency was supposed to send a letter to the lord directors of the company in Amsterdam. They in turn had to send the request to a subcommittee, and a year might go by before an answer was received in New Amsterdam. By that time the applicant would have given up on the chicken business and purchased a tavern instead.

The town had plenty of those. At one time there were seventeen public houses for a population of seven hundred, and drunken brawls were frequent. Even without liquor the citizens squabbled among themselves and with company officials who, everyone knew, misappropriated company funds.

Into this chaos strutted Peter ("Peg Leg") Stuyvesant in 1647 to take up his post as the fourth governor of New Netherland. His right leg had been crushed by a ball from a Spanish cannon in a naval battle he had led for the Dutch Republic. He was so proud of the wooden replacement that he had it encrusted with silver. Stuyvesant had a way of emphatically stumping with his peg as he walked as if to say, "I, Peter Stuyvesant, personification of the powerful Dutch West India Trading Company."

When apprised of the colony's sorry state, the lord directors wrote, "Treat the province like a tree which has been growing for some time and has run wild. It must be pruned with great care and bent with a tender hand to be brought in good shape."

Stuyvesant "pruned," but his hand was not tender.

He issued stringent rules against smuggling in order to stop the brisk black market that went on in the harbor and enacted laws to cut down on drinking. The drawing of a knife was punishable by a fine which was tripled if anyone was wounded. Stuyvesant also enforced the prohibition against selling arms and ammunition to the Indians. In one case he meted out a death sentence to an arms dealer guilty of this offense. (Under pressure by the townspeople, he later changed the sentence to banishment and confiscation of goods, and in the end only the last part was executed.) To remedy the ramshackle growth of the town, he appointed surveyors to "condemn all improper and disorderly buildings, fences, palisades, posts, rails." The New Amsterdammers didn't like Stuyvesant one bit.

In his own authoritarian way, Stuyvesant had the colony's best interests at heart. He sent letters to the lord directors for supplies of grain and agricultural tools and for more farmers and additional manpower for the town. The trading company, however, was not interested in colonizing because of the high initial costs and slow returns, and it did nothing to persuade the Dutch to go and settle in the New World, where the Dutch weren't keen to go in the first place. They had heard about the many company rules colonists had to follow, and the stories about wolves and "wild men" in the formidable American forests. And they knew all about the typhoid-ridden sailing vessels. For weeks, sometimes months, passengers were packed together in badly ventilated quarters below deck, where the frequent sprinkling of boiling vinegar could not defeat the smell of unwashed bodies, vomit, and bilge water. English Puritans might want to put up with such accommodations, but they were persecuted for their faith. The Dutch were not.

To alleviate the labor problem, the company sent fifty

boys and girls from Amsterdam almshouses, causing Stuyvesant to complain that most of them were "more inclined to carry a beggar gripsack than to labor." The experiment was not repeated.

Lack of colonists, people who came to stay and till the land, was one of the chief reasons for the fall of New Netherland.

The neighboring English didn't have to write home for grain; they grew it. They didn't have to ask for workers; they raised families. By 1664 the English outnumbered the Dutch by at least ten to one, and New Netherland had become a sore spot in English eyes. The king of England decided to take the eyesore away. Without even having conquered it, he gave the Dutch territory to his brother, the Duke of Albany and York. Four English men-of-war sailed into New Amsterdam to ask for surrender. Stuyvesant wanted to put up resistance, but the citizens did not agree with him. Maybe they thought that this was as good a time as any to cut themselves off from the meddling West India Company and to get rid of their harsh and demanding governor. There wasn't much to fight with anyway, because the town garrison consisted of barely one hundred fifty soldiers, and two hundred fifty citizens at the most knew how to use arms. So little powder was left that the fort's gunner said, "If I begin in the forenoon, 'twill all be consumed in the afternoon."

On September 8, 1664, thirty-eight years after the Dutch had bought Manhattan Island from the Indians, they gave up the best-situated harbor on the eastern seaboard along with thousands of acres of fertile plains and virgin forests. They briefly won part of the colony back from the English, but after 1675 New Netherland ceased to exist. New Amsterdam was called New York after the Duke of York, and his Albany title was bestowed on Fort Orange, which the Dutch had named after their national hero, William of Orange.

At the end of Dutch rule, the total European population of

New Netherland was an estimated eight to ten thousand, about two-thirds of whom were Dutch and many of them had been born in the colony.

Under English rule the Dutch continued to do business in New Amsterdam and to farm in the small Dutch-founded communities in the Hudson Valley, on western Long Island, and south of the Delaware River. As the frontier expanded, Dutch farmers founded communities in newly opened land.

It's ironic that while New Netherland failed partly because of lack of farmers, a hundred years later Dutch farmers were scattered all over the English colonies and praised as great improvers of the land. A traveling Frenchman noted that the farms of the average Dutchman of New York were the "neatest in all the country, and you will judge by his waggon and fat horses, that he thinks more of the affairs of this world than those of the next."

(The Frenchman meant Holland-Dutch farmers, not the Pennsylvania Dutch, who identified themselves upon arrival as *Deutsch*, which means German, and were often mistaken for Dutch—a confusion that reigns to this day.)

During the colonial period only a trickle of Dutch immigrants came over. The first big wave of twenty thousand crossed the Atlantic between 1840 and 1860.

One reason the Dutch now left home in large numbers was the search for a better life. By 1850, one-fourth of the Dutch population was unemployed. Floods inundated precious farmland patiently won from the water, and the potato blight that brought so many Irish to the United States also wreaked its havoc on The Netherlands.

Some left their homeland because they could not practice their religion as they pleased. The Seceders objected to a new law that made the king protector of the church and placed the church synods, classes, and consistories under government supervision. The Seceders also did not approve of modern ideas that had crept into church ritual, ideas which were "not according to Calvin." One such innovation was the singing of hymns other than the traditional psalms of David. Another was that the name of the church was changed from *gereformeerd*, a name in use for almost two hundred fifty years, to *hervormd*. Both words mean "reformed" and refer to the Protestant Reformation, but *hervormd* also means reorganized. Reorganized to suit the wishes of the king said the Seceders.

The Seceders left the church, but they were not allowed to form a new one. "The constitution of 1814 guarantees religious freedom to existing churches, not to new groups," said autocratic William I. He even forbade the Seceders to gather. When they did anyway, church ministers were arrested or fined. To break the Seceders' morale, nonbelieving and often obnoxious soldiers were billeted in their homes.

Under continual harassment the Seceders decided to move en masse to America. Emigrant societies were organized with charters that spelled out financial arrangements, conduct on board ship, and provisional governments in the new settlements. Scouts were sent ahead to prepare the way, and if possible, choose a settlement site.

When the Seceders left The Netherlands after years of planning, their difficulties had virtually stopped, and in 1848 a new constitution granted everyone freedom of worship. Nothing, however, could stop their momentum, and in later years, they could not say whether they had emigrated for religious or for economic reasons. In many instances the answer was both.

The group led by Dominie Albertus Christiaan van Raalte traveled to forested Michigan in 1847. "Our first task was to place sticks in the ground, cover them with bark of trees, gather leaves for our bed, and the house was ready," wrote one of the settlers. On the flat grassland of the old country no one had felled giant trees. In Michigan trees kept falling the wrong way. How to burn heavy stumps or roll them out of the way had to be learned, and to build a log cabin was a monumental task. Supplies had to come a long distance by ox team or on someone's back. Settlers became ill and died. Parents buried children with their own hands.

After the first difficult year, life started to improve. Seeds turned into crops and settlers built real houses. Craftsmen opened blacksmith and leather shops. Traders opened flour mills and banks. Holland, Michigan, became a prosperous town.

Dominie Hendrik Pieter Scholte led his group to the prairies of southeastern Iowa and founded Pella. Meaning refuge, Pella was also the name of a town to which Christians fled in A.D. 70, after the Romans had destroyed Jerusalem. Dominie Scholte favored the prairies because here his colony could avoid "the unusual battle with trees and the constant view of stumps in the midst of meadows and cultivated fields" that the Michigan settlers had to face.

A month after the group arrived in Iowa, a reporter for the local newspaper wrote, "I discovered a new race of beings . . . a broadshouldered race in velvet jackets and wooden shoes. . . . Most of the inhabitants live in camps, the tops covered with tent cloth, some with grass bushes. The sides barricaded with countless numbers of trunks, boxes, and chests of the oldest and most grotesque description that Yankees . . . ever beheld. . . . Their present population numbers something like 700 to 800 souls with the expectation of a numerous accession of numbers the ensuing spring. They appear to be intelligent and respectable."

The second big wave of Dutch immigration occurred during the 1880s when nearly 55,000 Dutch landed on American shores. The number was large only in comparison with earlier Dutch migrations. While 175,000 Dutch immigrated in the period between the Civil War and World War I, the total from other European countries was 25 million.

In the second wave were many followers, prompted by letters from relatives and friends already in the United States. The letters mentioned the cheap, fertile land and the pleasing social climate. "Everyone associates on a more equal level," one Dutch dominie wrote. "One who is somewhat ahead of others, because of intelligence and education, possessions and income, profession or position, does not allow himself to be very prominent."

The Dutch immigrants were also attracted by brochures circulated in The Netherlands by American railroad companies or real estate developers. A 36-page pamphlet published in 1883, *Land en Dollars in Minnesota: Inlichtingen voor Landverhuizers* ("Land and Dollars in Minnesota: Information for Emigrants"), gave information about the purchase of railroad and other lands, agricultural implements that would be needed, draft animals, and seeds. The pamphlet emphasized that poor Hollanders should not be discouraged from emigrating. "There are hundreds, no thousands, who began with nothing who are now independent. The idea that the far west is a haven of refuge for the poor is not an exaggeration. More important than money are good health, a pair of strong arms, temperance, thrift, and a firm will to go ahead."

With a firm will the great majority of these Dutch settlers did well, and the same can be said of the third big wave that arrived after World War II when the economic future of The Netherlands looked grim, and half a million Dutch emigrated to non-European countries.

Of this number, 86,997 came to the United States as of 1975. Some came under the annual "ethnic quota" of 3,136—a quota in effect from 1929 to 1965 when annual arrivals from each country were restricted to a number based on the ethnic composition of the American people as reflected in the population census of 1920. In 1953, however, the Refugee Relief Act authorized the issuance of 17,000 immigration visas to Dutch immigrants over and above this annual quota. Among those eligible were Dutch nationals of Dutch-Indonesian parentage who repatriated from the now independent Dutch colonies to The Netherlands only to find an alarming housing shortage and lack of work. In 1958 and 1960, the Walter-Pastore Acts I and II admitted 17,800 Dutch-Indonesians. Many of these chose to live in southern California, where the climate and vegetation reminded them of their tropical native land.

After three hundred fifty years of Dutch immigration, the Dutch presence is now very much part of the American scene.

The Midwest, where many Dutch-Americans still gather together, has its tulip festivals. Holland, Michigan, and Pella and Orange City, Iowa, draw thousands of springtime visitors, including many non-Dutch who delight in seeing the tulips along the streets, in parks, and in gardens. A festival day usually starts with a street inspection by the town mayor, who wears a wide-brimmed felt hat, silver-buttoned velvet jacket, and breeches for the occasion. The streets are always too dirty for His Honor, so men tote buckets of water hanging from wooden yokes while dozens of women and children in traditional dress scrub the streets in memory of their ancestors' mania for scrubbing stoops and sidewalks. The diverse origins of the immigrants is obvious. Scheveningen women wear boat-shaped bonnets with golden ear irons, Zeeland women have coifs as large as sails, and the peaked caps of the Volendam women curl at the edges.

In communities with many Dutch-Americans, there is bound to be a Dutch baker who sells the different kinds of freshly baked bread that the Dutch like to eat for their koffietafel. Dutch bakeries also carry imported chocolate sprinkles to put on the bread, spiced speculaas cookies in the shape of windmills, boxes of chocolate letters for the year-end holidays, and Indonesian spices for the Dutch-Indonesians so they can make *nasi goreng* ("fried rice") or even elaborate "rice tables."

On Sunday many Dutch-Americans meet in churches that are closely associated with the Dutch immigration. The Reformed Church of America, formerly the Dutch Reformed Church, was founded in 1628 in New Amsterdam. The Christian Reformed Church was founded in the Midwest in 1857 by Seceder immigrants who found the Dutch Reformed Church in their new homeland too reminiscent of the church from which they had just seceded. The founders of the new church believed strongly in Christian education, and it now sponsors numerous parent-controlled Christian primary and secondary schools. In Grand Rapids, Michigan, Calvin College combines a theological seminary with a four-year liberal arts college.

Although the individualistic Dutch are not joiners, there are clubs across the country that offer evenings of *klaverjas*, a Dutch card game, and a party on koninginnedag ("queen's day"), April 30. The queen's former subjects may sport an orange blouse or orange flower in the lapel. On December 5 a mitred and red-robed Saint Nicholas brings gifts for children. Before Christmas, club members, even those who never set foot in a church the rest of the year, go to church to sing Dutch Christmas carols.

The two largest Dutch clubs are AVIO, which stands for *Alle Vermaak is Ons* ("All Pleasure is Ours"), in Anaheim, California, with twenty-two hundred member families, and the Dutch Immigrant Society (DIS) in Grand Rapids, Michigan, with twelve thousand member families. Everyone is welcome in either club; the DIS expresses the hope on the application form that new members agree with the purpose and basis of the society, which is that "all things not only be done for the benefit of the members, but above all to the glory of God."

The only Dutch club that is difficult to join is the Holland Society of New York. Its male members have to be able to prove that they descend in the direct male line from a Dutchman who lived in New Netherland before 1675. Although the club's nine hundred fifty members are spread all over the United States, they try to meet once a year for an annual banquet. While business is conducted, the rostrum is graced by a stuffed beaver, the animal that drew the first Dutch to the New World.

Dutch-American organizations perpetuate the external trappings of the Dutch heritage, but it has also been self-perpetuated in another, more subtle way—through Dutch words, expressions with the word "Dutch," Dutch place names, and Dutch family names.

The American language has adopted Dutch words like yacht (*jacht*), coleslaw (*kool*, "cabbage," and *sla*, "salad"), skate (*schaats*), waffle (*wafel*), cookie (*koekje*), and golf after the Dutch game of *kolf* played on the ice. (It should be noted, however, that the Scots also claim credit for the word golf; they say that the game originated in Scotland.)

Expressions with the word "Dutch" are all rather derogatory, and the Dutch are sure they were introduced in New Netherland days by the English, who did not care much for their neighbors' pesky trading monopoly. "Dutch courage" is inspired by drinking liquor. When you "go Dutch," everyone pays his way. A "Dutch treat" similarly assumes that no one treats: you go fifty-fifty. To be "in Dutch with" means to be in disfavor with. To talk "double Dutch" is to talk gibberish. A "Dutch uncle" criticizes with unsparing severity.

In New York, Wall Street reminds us of the *wal* surrounding the fortress in New Amsterdam. The Bowery is called after the *bouwerij,* the farm where Peter Stuyvesant lived out his life. Brooklyn takes its name from the New Netherland town of Breukelen. Yonkers was the estate of a Dutchman of gentlemanly birth, called a *jonkheer* in Dutch.

Take a phone book of any American city, and you are likely to find names starting with *De* (De Boer, De Bruin—sometimes written DeBoer, DeBruin) and *Van* (Van Dongen, Van Dijk—sometimes spelled Dyk).

If you go to a bookstore or the library, you will also find names of well-known authors that start with *De* or *Van.* Paul de Kruif, who was born of Dutch parents in Zeeland, Michigan, wrote *The Microbe Hunters* (1926), a book about pioneers in bacteriology that is still in print. Hendrik Willem Van Loon, an immigrant to this country in 1903, wrote *The Story of the Bible* (1923) and *The Story of Mankind* (1926). Jan de Hartog, author of *Hollands Glorie,* a classic Dutch novel about an ocean-going tugboat captain, has written plays and books in English, including a saga about the Quakers, *The Peaceable Kingdom* (1971). De Hartog settled in the United States after World War II.

Meindert DeJong, born in 1910 behind the big sea dike in Wierum, Friesland, and now residing in Michigan, not only has his thoroughly Dutch name on the covers of his books for children, but he also brings his delightful experiences as a Dutch child to life for young American readers. *The Tower by the Sea* (1950) is based on the legend he heard as a boy about the cat who kept a cradle afloat during Saint Elizabeth's flood in 1421. *The Wheel on the School* (1954) recounts the efforts of young Frisians to get a stork to nest in their village and has been translated into Frisian. *Journey from Peppermint Street* (1968) is the tale of a nine-year-old boy's adventures away from home, vividly punctuated by the description of a breach in the dike.

Stories for younger children are written and illustrated by Peter Spier, the son of the Dutch artist Jo Spier, whose illustrated books are collector's items in The Netherlands. *The Legend of New Amsterdam* (1979), the latest of Peter Spier's sixteen books, is dedicated to his father. It shows the Dutch people and their children in whimsical renderings of colonial city life in 1660.

The Dutch language spoken in immigrant homes and churches was not at first considered an object of study. Now, however, there are several academic programs. Columbia University in New York has had the Queen Wilhelmina Chair of History, Language, and Literature of The Netherlands since 1913 with the financial assistance of the Dutch government. In 1953 Calvin College created a professorship known as the Queen Juliana Chair of Dutch Language and Culture—after the Dutch monarch reigning at the time. And in 1971 the University of California at Berkeley was endowed with the Princess Beatrix Chair of Dutch Language, Literature, and Culture, named after Juliana's daughter.

UC Berkeley is the only university in the United States that has a degree program in Dutch studies (B.A.). The school offers a variety of graduate and undergraduate courses, including Dutch literature in the Golden Age, literature from the eighteenth to the twentieth century, Dutch painters, Erasmus of Rotterdam, and, of course, the Dutch language.

At least twenty other American colleges and universities offer courses in the Dutch language since students find a knowledge of Dutch helpful in doing research on colonialism, urban planning, and art history.

In seeking out the Dutch heritage in the United States, it is tempting to rummage about in search of great figures of Dutch descent. But how Dutch were they when they made their contributions? Were they who they were because of their Dutch ancestry or because of their American experience?

President Theodore Roosevelt gave an answer in 1890 in an address before the Holland Society of New York:

We of the Holland blood of New York have just cause to be proud of the men of note in American history who have come from among us . . . [but] the point on which I wish to insist is, that the Hollanders could never have played such a part, could never have won honorable renown by doing their full share in shaping the destiny of the republic, had they remained Hollanders instead of becoming Americans. . . . Had they remained aliens in speech and habit of thought, Schuyler would have been a mere boorish provincial squire instead of a major general in the Revolutionary army, Van Buren would have been a country tavern-keeper instead of the President of the mightiest republic the world has ever seen, and Vanderbilt would have remained an unknown boatman instead of becoming one of the most potent architects of the marvelous American industrial fabric.

OF ANTHEM, FLAG, AND KNIGHTS

IN THE "WILHELMUS," officially made the national anthem in 1932, the Dutch sing about Prince William of Orange honoring the king of Spain. The song was written during the Eighty Years War, probably by William's nobleman friend, Marnix van Sint Aldegonde, in 1568 or thereabouts, when William had not yet broken with his feudal sovereign, King Philip II of Spain. At the time William was still hoping to achieve independence for The Netherlands without forsaking his sovereign "given by God."

The song's fifteen verses extol the virtues and the ideals of William, and each one starts with a letter of "Willem van Nassov," the county of Nassau being another of William's properties. Only the first and sometimes the sixth verse are sung whenever there is occasion to sing the national anthem.

> Wilhelmus van Nassouwe
> Ben ick van Dietschen bloet;
> Den Vaderlant ghetrouwe
> Blijf ick tot in den doet.
> Een prince van Oranjen
> Ben ick vrij onverveert;
> Den Coninck van Hispanjen
> Heb ik altijd ghe-eert.
>
> Mijn schild en de betrouwen
> Sijt ghy, o Godt, mijn Heer!
> Op U so wil ick bouwen,
> Verlaat mij nimmermeer!
> Dat ick doch vroom mach blijven,
> U dienaer t'allerstont,
> Die tyranny verdrijven,
> Die mij mijn hert doorwont.

(This Dutch spelling is not in use anymore.)

The anthem translates into English as:

> William of Nassau,
> Scion of a Dutch and ancient line,
> I dedicate undying faith
> To this land of mine.
> A prince I am, undaunted,
> Of Orange, ever free.
> To the King of Spain
> I've granted lifelong loyalty.
>
> A shield and my reliance
> O God, Thou ever wert.
> I'll trust unto Thy guidance.
> Do leave me not ungirt
> That I may stay a pious
> Servant of Thine for aye
> And drive the plagues that try us
> And tyranny away.

The Dutch tend to sing the anthem slowly, as if they were singing a hymn in church.

Prince William was also the force behind the national flag. The red, white, and blue horizontal stripes are a variation of the stripes on the rebels' flag during the sixteenth-century insurrection. The stripes were then orange, white, and blue—colors taken from William's coat of arms.

It should be noted that the Frisians have a national flag of their own. It is blue and cut by three diagonal white bands broken by seven heart-shaped red water lily leaves. Naturally, the Frisians also have their own national anthem.

The French motto of the now royal Orange family's coat of arms, *Je Maintiendrai* ("I shall maintain"), is on the emblem of The Netherlands. It consists of a gold lion rampant, who holds in his right paw a silver Roman sword with golden hilt and in his left paw a sheaf of seven gold-tipped silver arrows. The animal is shown against a background of azure.

Furthermore, the Oranges created the three Dutch orders of the knighthood: the Military Order of William, the Order of the Netherlands Lion (both instituted by King William I in 1815), and the Order of Orange-Nassau, which dates from 1892.

Ranks in the Military Order of William, awarded for a combination of fine personal qualities in time of war, are given the least frequently. The order has four degrees: bearer of the grand cross, commander, knight of the third degree, and knight of the fourth degree. Quite a few of these decorations were awarded after World War II to military personnel and resistance workers for their valiant wartime efforts.

The decoration of the Order of Orange Nassau, which has five degrees, is sometimes given out to foreigners. Americans who have received the highest rank recently are General Alexander M. Haig, Jr., former head of NATO in Europe, and Admiral Isaac C. Kidd, Supreme Allied Commander of the Atlantic. Both men received the Grand Cross of Orange-Nassau "with the swords" because they are in the military.

Annually, hundreds of Dutch receive lower decorations in this order for contributions to the cultural and socioeconomic life of The Netherlands and meritorious service in government. The government officials are listed by department in the newspapers when the queen awards the decorations on koninginnedag. The papers talk about the *lintjesregen* ("the rain of little ribbons"). The *lintjes,* like the "fruit salad" of the American military, are the outward signs of the honors.

The owners of the little ribbons can wear them whenever they wish, but they usually do so only for festive occasions or official receptions. The ribbons, sometimes twisted into a tiny cockade, have different colors, and only the initiated know what rank of which order a ribbon represents. If you are curious about it, it is all right to ask.

USEFUL ADDRESSES

In The Netherlands

Royal Dutch Touring Club ANWB
Wassenaarseweg 220
P.O. Box 93200
2509 BA The Hague
Telephone: (070)-264426
(Information on membership,
maps, and bicycle events)

De Hollandsche Molen
(Foundation for the Preservation of
Windmills in The Netherlands)
Prins Hendrikkade 108
1011 AK Amsterdam

Netherlands War Graves Committee
Josuëlaan 2
H. Landstichting
6564 BE post Nijmegen

NRC Handelsblad
P.O. Box 824
3000 DL Rotterdam
(Newspaper with weekly airmail edition)

NUFFIC (Netherlands Universities
Foundation for International Cooperation)
Badhuisweg 251
P.O. Box 90734
2509 LS The Hague

De Porceleyne Fles
Royal Delftware
Rotterdamseweg 196
P.O. Box 11
2600 AA Delft

The Royal Netherlands League
for Physical Culture (KNBLO)
Valkenbosplein 18
2563 CB The Hague
(Information on four-day distance march)

Scheltema, Holkema & Vermeulen, B.V.
Spuistraat 10A
1012 WZ Amsterdam
(To order books)

Stichting Friese 11-steden Wandeltochten
P.O. Box 945
8901 BS Leeuwarden
(Information on six-day Friesland walk)

Strandzesdaagse
P.O. Box 299
1780 AG Den Helder
(Information on six-day beach walk)

Tichelaars Royal Makkum
Earthenware and Tile Factory
P.O. Box 11
8754 ZN Makkum

VVV Gelderland
P.O. Box 552
6800 AN Arnhem
(Information on
"packaged" bicycle tours)

VVV Leeuwarden/Friesland
Stationsplein 1
8911 AC Leeuwarden
(Information about hiking on tidal flats)

Wadloopcentrum
Hoofdstraat 68
9968 AG Pieterburen
(Information about hiking on tidal flats)

Outside The Netherlands

Dutch Club AVIO, Inc.
1557 West Katella Avenue
Anaheim, California 92802

Dutch Immigrant Society
1239 East Fulton
P.O. Box 6462
Grand Rapids, Michigan 49506

Frisian Information Bureau
1229 Sylvan Avenue SE
Grand Rapids, Michigan 49506

Netherlands National Tourist Office
476 Fifth Avenue
New York, New York 10036

Netherlands National Tourist Office
681 Market Street, Room 941
San Francisco, California 94105

Netherlands National Tourist Office
Toronto Dominion Centre
P.O. Box 311
Toronto, Ontario M5K 1K2
Canada

The Windmill Herald
Vanderheide Publishing Co., Ltd.
P.O. Box 533
New Westminster, B.C. V3L 4Y8
Canada
(Appears twice a month with news
in Dutch about The Netherlands)

SELECTED BIBLIOGRAPHY

Bird, R.B. and W.Z. Schetter. *Een Goed Begin: A Contemporary Dutch Reader,* 2d rev. ed. The Hague: Martinus Nijhoff, 1974.

Boxer, C.R. *The Dutch Seaborne Empire, 1600–1800.* London: Hutchinson, 1965.

de Jong, Gerald F. *The Dutch in America, 1609–1974.* Boston: Twayne Publishers, 1975.

Fuchs, R.H. *Dutch Painting.* New York: Oxford University Press, 1978.

Goudsblom, Johan. *Dutch Society.* Philadelphia: Philadelphia Books Co., 1966.

Irving, Washington. *A History of New York from the Beginning of the World to the End of the Dutch Dynasty.* Edited by Edwin T. Bowden. New Haven: College and University Press, 1964. A lighthearted satire.

Meijer, R.P. *Literature of the Low Countries.* New York: Irvington Publications, 1978.

Michelin Red Guide to Benelux: Belgium, Netherlands, Luxembourg. Paris: Michelin Tire, 1979. Updated regularly.

Shetter, William Z. *Introduction to Dutch: A Practical Grammar.* The Hague: Martinus Nijhoff, 1977.

————. *The Pillars of Society: Six Centuries of Civilization in The Netherlands.* The Hague: Martinus Nijhoff, 1971.

van der Zee, Henri and Barbara. *A Sweet and Alien Land: The Story of the Dutch in New York.* New York: Viking Press, 1978.

In the United States, a bookseller can probably procure any of the above books, all of which were still in print as of 1980. Those listed below can best be ordered through a bookstore in The Netherlands. An American bookseller may be able to help out, or you can order direct from a book importer. W.S. Heinman (1966 Broadway, New York, New York 10023) specializes in books from The Netherlands.

de Hartog, Jan. *Hollands Glorie.* Amsterdam: Elsevier, 1944. A novel about ocean-going tugboats.

de Jong, L. *Fragmenten uit het Koninkrijk der Nederlanden in de Tweede Wereldoorlog: a. De Jaren '30; b. De Duitse Invasie; c. De Jodenvervolging I; d. Het Illegale Werk; e. Nederlandse Unie; f. Begin van het England-spiel; g. Jodenvervolging II; h. Vier Portretten.* The Hague: Staatsuitgeverij, 1977, 1978. Eight pocket books which are condensations of a much larger, definitive work on World War II.

Dekker, Eduard Douwes [Multatuli]. *Max Havelaar.* Rotterdam: Ad. Donker, 1958. A reprint with modernized spelling of an 1860 novel about abuses in the Dutch colonies.

den Doolaard, A. *Het Verjaagde Water.* Amsterdam: Em. Querido's Uitgeverij, 1948. A novel about the 1944 flood in Walcheren.

de Rek, J. *Koningen Kabinetten en Klompenvolk.* 2 vols. Baarn: Bosch & Keunig N.V., 1975, 1978.

———. *Prinsen Patriciërs en Patriotten.* Baarn: Bosch & Keunig N.V., 1967.

———. *Van Boergondië tot Barok.* Baarn: Bosch & Keunig N.V., 1967.

———. *Van Hunebed tot Hanzestad.* Baarn: Bosch & Keunig N.V., 1954.

Jacobs, Aletta H. *Herinneringen.* 1926. Reprint. Nijmegen: Sun, 1978.

Romein, Jan and Annie. *Erflaters van Onze Beschaving.* 9th rev. ed. Amsterdam: Em. Querido's Uitgeverij, 1971.

———. *De Lage Landen bij de Zee.* 5th rev. ed. Amsterdam: Em. Querido's Uitgeverij, 1973.

Romein-Verschoor, Annie. *Vaderland in de Verte*. Amsterdam: Em. Querido's Uitgeverij, 1948. A novel about Hugo de Groot.

Stokhuyzen, Frederick. *The Dutch Windmill*. Bussum: C.A.J. van Dishoek, 1962.

Uit in Eigen Land: Vijftig Toeristische Tochten in Nederland. 2d rev. ed. Amsterdam: Uitgeversmaatschappij The Readers Digest, 1979.

ACKNOWLEDGMENTS

A *"heel hartelijk dank!"* ("heartfelt thanks") goes to the staff members of Dutch government offices, tourist associations, sporting organizations, broadcasting companies, industrial corporations, and historical societies, who answered questions, sent information and documentation, or granted me an interview when I was in The Netherlands.

I also want to thank the following persons who read part of the manuscript and offered valuable suggestions. They are listed here with their academic titles, as is the Dutch custom, their names alphabetized without "van" or "de." The names of married women appear with their maiden names included. Fr. Ackermans in Schin-op-Geul; E. W. Berg of the National Service of the IJsselmeer-polders in Lelystad; Ir. M. V. E. Bongaerts of DHV Consulting Engineers in Amersfoort; C. J. Canters in Poortvliet, co-author of *Wereld in Wording* ("A Growing World"), a series of high school history books; J. C. van Dalsen and Liduine Th. A. Hoyinck of the Provincial VVV Gelderland in Arnhem; Mr. Drs. C. G. van Geest, consul-general of The Netherlands in San Francisco; Beate Gleistein and Gerda W. S. Mus of the Educational Service of the National Gallery in Amsterdam; C. A. van Hees of "The Dutch Windmill" in Amsterdam; W. Hoffman in Vught; Matthey Hove-stadt of the provincial VVV Zeeland in Middelburg; Professor Dr. L. de Jong of the National Institute for War Documentation in Amsterdam; Joke Klosters of the provincial VVV Drenthe in

Assen; G. F. Kooijman of the Friesland/Leeuwarden VVV in Leeuwarden; G. H. V. van Lijf of the VVV in Maastricht; Drs. H. Meijer of the Geographic Institute of the University of Utrecht; my cousins Dr. N. E. van de Poll and Drs. N. P. van de Poll-Heyning in Blaricum; Mr. S. H. Poppema of the Ministry of Education and Science in The Hague (who pointed out that his favorable comments on the text did not constitute an authorization by his department); Stephanie Pressman, California poet and writer; Mr. K. Th. M. van Rijckevorsel, member of the Council of State in The Hague; Lucy I. Sargeant, California painter; A. A. Schaafsma of the Ministry of Water and Transport in The Hague; Drs. Nel Schokking who taught me English at the Christian Gymnasium of The Hague (now Sorghvliet Gymnasium); Professor Dr. J. P. Snapper, Head of the Princess Beatrix Chair of Dutch Language, Literature, and Culture at the University of California at Berkley; and my son-in-law and daughter, Drs. Th. P. Tromp and Drs. M. F. Tromp-van Rijckevorsel.

And I'd like to give a special thank-you to Linda P. Kusserow, senior editor at Dillon Press, who counseled, criticized, and cheered during many months of correspondence between Minneapolis and Menlo Park.

The photographs are reproduced courtesy of Helen Colijn; Galleria Nazionale d'Arte Antica, Rome; International Bulb Center, Hillegom; Magazijn *De Bijenkorf* B. V. and Frits Weideman, Photographer; National Gallery, Amsterdam; Port of Rotterdam; and the United States Army.

The poem "Thinking of Holland" by Hendrik Marsman is reproduced by permission of Em. Querido's Uitgeverij N.V. and W. van Hoeve, Ltd.

INDEX